A Pictorial History 1940–1975
WEBER & DAVIS COUNTIES

Presented by the Standard-Examiner and Ogden Union Station

Acknowledgments

The volume you hold in your hands is much more than a history book.

It's really a time machine.

The pictures on its pages have the power to transport you to the 1940s, '50s, '60s and '70s to watch as Weber and Davis counties grew from adolescents to adults.

Most of the photos come from the collections of local citizens who waited patiently at Ogden's Union Station for their turn to share their pictures—and their memories—with you.

Union Station Librarian Lee Witten and Jason Rusch, a Union Station volunteer and employee of the Weber County Library, deserve special recognition. Lee and Jason searched through literally suitcases filled with photos to find the gems reprinted on these pages.

Associate Curator Sarah Langsdon of Weber State also deserves thanks. Photos from Special Collections at the university's Stewart Library completed these pages.

Charles Trentelman was asked once again to write the foreword and chapter introductions. Charles brought the same care and craftsmanship to the text of this book as he did when he authored the history of the "Early Years" of Weber County. Features Editor Vanessa Zimmer once again edited his work.

Sources:

"A History of Davis County," by Glen M. Leonard. Published 1999 by the Utah State Historical Society.

"History of Hill Air Force Base." Published 1981 by the history office, Ogden Air Logistics Center, Hill Air Force Base.

"Ogden City, its Governmental Legacy," by G. Ross Peterson & Robert Parsons. Published 2001 by Chapelle Ltd., Ogden.

"Weber County's History," by Richard Roberts and Richard Sadler. Published 2000 by the Weber County Commission.

"Ogden Rails: A History of Railroads in Ogden, Utah From 1869 to Today," by Don Strack. Published 1997 in association with the Golden Spike Chapter, Railway & Locomotive Historical Society, Ogden.

Files of the *Standard-Examiner*.

Files of the *Davis County Clipper*.

Utah Digital Newspapers, J. Willard Marriott Library, University of Utah.

Contents

Foreword

Some perspective is in order to appreciate the pictures you are about to enjoy.

The time period beginning 1940 marks not just the start of World War II, but also the transformation of Weber and Davis counties.

Before, both counties were agricultural areas.

Weber County had railroads, but its industry centered on canning, slaughterhouses and food processing.

Davis County, with just 3,400 people, was Utah's breadbasket. There was so little else that, in 1896, Simon Bamberger, building a passenger train north, put up a resort near Farmington so people would have a reason to ride. Lagoon, a major Davis tourism attraction, survives today.

In the 1930s, fighting the Depression, the Top of Utah's business leaders saw preparations for war as a chance to attract new industry and jobs.

When the government sniffed around Utah to build an air base, the Ogden Chamber of Commerce acted. It bought options on 4,265 acres of land 10 miles south of the city, near an ammunition depot called the Ogden Arsenal. Then it waited patiently until the federal government came up with money to buy it. The Chamber donated 386 acres of land outright, and what is now Hill Air Force Base was born.

North of Ogden, the Utah General Depot, later Defense Depot Ogden, was planned. Congress appropriated $310,000 for the 1,679 acres, which were appraised at $409,632. In 48 hours, the Ogden Chamber came up with the additional $100,000.

Construction of the Clearfield Naval Depot began June 25, 1942, according to the *Davis County Clipper*:

"Prior to that time, there had been much controversy concerning the selection of the site, but patriotic farmers yielded to the desire of our government and gave up their lands and homes."

More than $100 million, equal to $1.5 billion today, was spent building these three facilities. Employment topped 52,000, equal to the state's entire agricultural industry and 50 percent more than all Utah manufacturing at the time.

Whole cities sprang up to house workers and their families. The first hints of suburban sprawl could be seen.

Those people didn't just work, of course. They danced to big bands, went to shows and participated in sports. They formed service clubs, went to church and shopped at the corner grocery. They built roads, water systems, schools.

And always, someone had a camera handy.

Everyone would line up, someone would holler "Say cheese!" and we can still see those smiling people today.

Well, they should be smiling. Look around at their handiwork. If you like where you live, thank them.

Charles F. Trentelman
Standard-Examiner

CHAPTER ONE

Views & Street Scenes

In the late 1940s, when Ogden photographer Larry Carr was a youngster, he and his family would go to Lagoon on the Bamberger railroad.

His family lived on 17th Street in Ogden. The Bamberger station was on 24th, so they'd walk down, hauling an old beer box to serve as a picnic table.

The trains, he said, were "rattly old things with their wooden benches. They weren't built for comfort.

"I remember going through Roy and Sunset, and I thought, 'What exotic names!' This is when I was 8 or 10," he said. "And the thing that stands out in my mind is, they were mostly open fields."

Through most of the 1950s and 1960s, Davis County's main business was either growing stuff or doing business with the folks who grew stuff.

Layton and Farmington had central business districts, but they were small, homey, the sorts of places one could sit in front of the courthouse, watch the cars go by and discuss seed prices.

Farther north was Ogden.

Ogden, the state's second largest city, was the "big city," with theaters and restaurants, shops and department stores.

A person having a day on the town could have lunch at the Snappy Service Cafe, buy a suit and get a haircut at the Fred M. Nye department store, take in a show at the Egyptian and finish off with dancing at the Berthana.

Then go home and catch "The Phil Silvers Show." Maybe even see Rosemary Clooney singing in color, but only if a rich friend — the first color Motorola set cost $1,295 in 1954, or $9,934 in 2007 dollars — let the neighbors come over and watch.

Pricey, sure, but Rosemary was worth every penny.

■ **LEFT:** Lift at Snow Basin, summer 1947.
Courtesy of Special Collections Department, Stewart Library, Weber State University

■ **RIGHT:** State School for the Deaf and Blind.
Courtesy of Special Collections Department, Stewart Library, Weber State University

■ **ABOVE:** Ogden Canyon, circa 1942. *Courtesy of Jean Sutherland*

■ **LEFT:** View of Ogden grain elevators, circa 1940.
Courtesy of Special Collections Department, Stewart Library, Weber State University

■ **ABOVE LEFT:** New Weber campus site of the student union building, "Hall of Yearning." *Courtesy of Special Collections Department, Stewart Library, Weber State University*

■ **ABOVE:** St. Benedict's from Ogden High School, October 1945.

Courtesy of Special Collections Department, Stewart Library, Weber State University

■ **RIGHT:** El Monte Golf Course, looking east toward Ogden Canyon, circa 1945.

Courtesy of Ogden Union Station Collection 2309

■ **ABOVE:** Washington Boulevard, looking east, circa 1948.

Courtesy of Ogden Union Station Collection 1983-6

■ **LEFT:** Looking up Washington Boulevard toward the business district, circa 1945.

Courtesy of Special Collections Department, Stewart Library, Weber State University

■ **RIGHT:** Dam at Camp Kiesel, June 13, 1948.
Courtesy of Jason Rusch

■ **BELOW RIGHT:** Edgehill Dairy on the edge of Ogden, January 1948.
Courtesy of Special Collections Department, Stewart Library, Weber State University

■ **BELOW:** Sign at North Junction, June 1948.
Courtesy of Special Collections Department, Stewart Library, Weber State University

■ **ABOVE:** Looking north on Washington Boulevard during the holidays, circa 1950. *Courtesy of Jason Rusch*

■ **BELOW:** Weber River flood, U.S. 89, George Kendell's Junction, May 1952. *Courtesy of T. Neil Dye*

■ **ABOVE:** Ogden Canyon, winter 1951. *Courtesy of Betty White*

■ **LEFT:** Ogden rail yards, looking east, circa 1960.
Courtesy of Ogden Union Station Collection 5268

■ **BELOW:** A rainy day on Washington Boulevard, circa 1968.
Courtesy of Ogden Union Station Collection 5518

■ **ABOVE:** 25th Street and Wall Avenue, looking east, 1965.
Courtesy of Ogden Union Station Collection

■ **LEFT:** Looking west down 25th Street, circa 1972. *Courtesy of Ogden Union Station Collection 5101*

CHAPTER TWO

Commerce & Industry

Prewar efforts to attract military installations to the Top of Utah paid off in the 1950s when the area faced a double whammy: the decline of agriculture and the decline of military jobs.

The history of the Naval Supply Depot in Clearfield illustrates what happened.

The depot was built in 1943 to meet two criteria: room for vast amounts of warehouse space to serve military needs on the West Coast via railroad, and safety from enemy attack.

The depot, built in 10 months and 22 days, was massive: 58 warehouses with 159 million cubic feet of space, 30 miles of railroad including 145 switches and 80,000 ties, 30 miles of roads and 18 miles of storm drains.

It employed thousands of people, including Italian prisoners of war. The depot provided support for naval aviation, cruisers, destroyers, medical stores, ordnance, PT boats and radar.

After the war, all of that went away. By 1963, the base had fewer than 2,000 workers and was struggling to justify itself.

It found an answer in private industries looking for warehouse space, coupled with a "freeport" law approved by the Utah Legislature in 1963.

The freeport law exempted items stored in Utah from property taxes if they were to be shipped out of the state again. The Freeport Center, as a national trans-shipment point, was born.

More than 70 companies currently use the Freeport Center to both manufacture and distribute. The center has 78 warehouses with more than 7 million square feet of space and, collectively, is one of Davis County's largest employers.

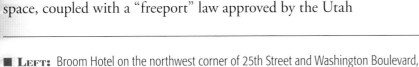

■ **LEFT:** Broom Hotel on the northwest corner of 25th Street and Washington Boulevard, circa 1940. Walgreen Drugs occupied its lower level in the 1940s and 1950s. *Courtesy of Jason Rusch*

■ **RIGHT:** The Oaks in Ogden Canyon, summer 1940. *Courtesy of Jack W. Gibbons*

■ **ABOVE LEFT:** Star Noodle Parlor at 265 25th St., circa 1945. The proprietor was Mrs. N. Kitamura.
Courtesy of Jason Rusch

■ **ABOVE RIGHT:** Jack W. Gibbons, age 15, worked as a carhop at The Oaks during the summer of 1940.
Courtesy of Jack W. Gibbons

■ **BELOW:** E. J. Fjeldsted standing in George B. Taylor's onions felds, Farr West, Oct. 26, 1944. Taylor had 11 acres, with production of 900 sacks per acre, 100 pounds per sack.
Courtesy of Special Collections Department, Stewart Library, Weber State University

■ **ABOVE:** Volunteer workers at the canning plant tackling tomatoes, June 10, 1943. The volunteers kept the plant going during the war years. From left to right: Mrs. Wesley Tomlinson, Mrs. P. B. Piersanti and Mrs. Eugene E. Snyder, all affiliates of the Ogden Elks Does. *Courtesy of Ogden Union Station Collection*

Right: Group at Porters and Waiters Club, circa 1945. Left to right: James Turner, Mac Henery, Tony White and Lloyde Cope.

Courtesy of Ogden Union Station Collection 0248

Below: Camp Cucumber's tomatoes in Davis County, spring 1945.

Courtesy of Special Collections Department, Stewart Library, Weber State University

Above: Fred M. Nye Co. just prior to opening a new store at 2422 Washington Blvd., circa 1940. It was previously located across the street in the Eccles Building.

Courtesy of Jason Rusch

Above: Spotlight King, a waiter at the Porters and Waiters Club, circa 1945.

Courtesy of Ogden Union Station Collection 0250

■ **FACING PAGE:** Tomato field at the Johnson farm in Hooper, circa 1945.

Courtesy of Special Collections Department, Stewart Library, Weber State University

■ **RIGHT:** Baling hay, 1945. In the center is Orville Holmes. The boys in front are Mont, left, and Sherm Holmes.

Courtesy of Lois Holmes Huston

■ **FAR RIGHT:** Women harvesting Randall's tomato crop in North Ogden, circa 1945.

Courtesy of Special Collections Department, Stewart Library, Weber State University

■ **BOTTOM RIGHT:** Sugar storage, Amalgamated Sugar Company, Ogden, November 1945.

Courtesy of Special Collections Department, Stewart Library, Weber State University

■ **BELOW:** Navajos working the beet fields in Weber County, circa 1948.

Courtesy of Special Collections Department, Stewart Library, Weber State University

■ ABOVE: Cherry pickers in North Ogden, June 1946. *Courtesy of Special Collections Department, Stewart Library, Weber State University*

■ **Above:** Huntsville businesses, circa 1955. From front to back: McKay's Grocery and Confectionery; Shooting Star Saloon, the oldest ongoing saloon in the state of Utah; a garage and service station; and the telephone office. *Courtesy of Doug and Erma Wilson*

■ **Left:** Utah Power and Light lobby in Ogden, circa 1952. Public interest was high as television made its debut in Ogden. Majestic TV Sales & Service Co. brought its television sets to display. Carolyn Saam, age 8, is seated on the floor with her lollipop. Her uncle, Roy Critchlow, worked at the power company. *Courtesy of Carolyn Saam Bennion*

■ **Top left:** J&K Drive-In, 4th Street and Washington Boulevard, was owned by Vernice Adams, 1950. The "J" and "K" stood for the names of her two children, Farrel J. and Kay. Known by the carhops as "Mrs. A.," Vernice would make sure all of the girls had a ride home after work in her Cadillac, or if she was unavailable her teenage son Farrel drove them home in his red convertible, stopping by KLO radio station where announcer Len Allen would get a complimentary malt. Known to have the best root beer around, and served in ice cold mugs, J&K was the hot spot to be after the Little Brown Jug game between Weber and Ogden high schools and was a favorite for teenagers "dragging the Boulevard." *Courtesy of Farrel J. Adams*

■ **LEFT:** American Can Company's 50th anniversary at White City Ballroom, circa 1949. Included in the group are Grant Hansen, who worked for American Can for 31 years, and Vera Roundy, who retired from the company.

Courtesy of Marilyn B. Hansen and Courtesy of Terry Roundy

■ **BELOW:** Park-N-Snack, 2735 Washington Blvd., circa 1955. *Courtesy of Jason Rusch*

■ **ABOVE:** Opening day of Sam and Ethel Harrop's new barbershop at 418 28th St., April 1956.

Courtesy of Jodi Jude Bobillot

■ **RIGHT:** Becker's Brewery, 1900 Lincoln Ave., Nov. 28, 1953. *Courtesy of Ogden Union Station Collection 1504*

■ **BELOW:** Safeway store on Washington Boulevard, circa 1955.

Courtesy of Ogden Union Station Collection 5394

■ **BOTTOM:** Royal McBee Printing Company Western Plant, 124 22nd St., 1955. Employees include Vern Hill, Duane Rogers, Les Cunningham, Vernon Taylor, LeRoy Rackham, Chuck Abbott, Jane Markland, Vern Harrop, Jack Gibbons, Jim Neeley, Gene Pilgrim, Dave Ballingham, Elda Whitlock, Janet Hancock, Ogilvie Cottrell, Winnifred Wadman, J. Howard Wadman, Sarah Loveday, Tom O'Malley, Jack Finder, Fred Hart, Harold Bell and John Boyd. Managers were Jim Widman and, later, Mr. Stimpson. *Courtesy of Jerry Harrop*

■ **ABOVE:** Inside the Safeway store on Washington Boulevard, circa 1955. *Courtesy of Ogden Union Station Collection 5394*

■ **Above:** American Can Company employees, 1959. Vera Roundy is in the second row, centered on the sign. Francine Clifton is eighth from the right in the second row; Harold Clifton is eighth from the right in the front row. *Courtesy of Terry Roundy*

■ **Above:** City View Dairy Farm cash and carry store, 4811 South Harrison, 1958. It was owned by Frank and Gerrit Wolthuis. Their slogan was "If it's City View, it's best for you!" At that time, milk was 74 cents a gallon, 20 cents a quart. Greenspot Orangeade was two gallons for a dollar. Behind the dairy was the milking parlor, which was showcased in several dairy equipment magazines as the most modern in Utah.
Courtesy of Paul Tex and Lynnette Hancock

■ **Left:** Brown's Ice Cream Co., 2551 Grant Ave., circa 1962. *Courtesy of Ogden Union Station Collection 1654*

■ **Above:** Boyles furniture store, circa 1975. *Courtesy of Leslie Cole*

■ **Left:** Looking north down Washington Boulevard in 1957. *Courtesy of Robert J. Parker*

CHAPTER THREE

Transportation

The end of World War II saw the Top of Utah still using the transportation system of the 1930s, but that would not last.

Ogden's system of trolley cars had been replaced by buses in 1935, but the Bamberger still carried passengers along the Wasatch Front.

But look at the pictures in this chapter.

The train and railroad facilities have an old and worn look. Railroads didn't have money in the 1950s to modernize because passenger traffic had plunged.

Now look at the automobiles: They are sleek, streamlined, modern.

Look who owns the cars.

Before, cars were, for the most part, owned by the well-to-do, the city's bankers and businessmen. Here, regular folks have cars. The local dealerships employ dozens of people. Cars are everywhere, driven by everyone.

It was the time of America's love affair with the car. Dignitaries at the 75th anniversary of the driving of the golden spike for the transcontinental railroad had no idea they were celebrating an industry in decline.

Bamberger's final electric trains ran between Ogden and Salt Lake City on Sept. 6, 1952. By 1962, the *Standard-Examiner* was running regular stories on the building of interstate highways through Davis and Weber counties, eating up farmland as they went.

"Super highways of the future gradually taking shape today across the nation to connect cities, towns and the ever-diminishing farmlands will soon be curving their smooth, four-lane stretches into the Ogden area," reads one story.

Bamberger's rails were ripped out and Union Pacific's passenger trains dwindled to nothing. By 1975, the first subdivisions in Davis County were crossing city planners' desks, and the urban boom was on.

All driven by cars.

■ **LEFT:** Union Station on the 82nd anniversary of the Golden Spike, 1951. The station was rebuilt and completed in 1924.

Courtesy of Special Collections Department, Stewart Library, Weber State University

■ **RIGHT:** Showroom of Hunter Motor Company, 359 26th St., 1941.

Courtesy of Ogden Union Station Collection

■ **ABOVE:** Employees of the Utah Army Defense Depot on their way to work in May 1943. They rode from Preston, Idaho, to Ogden on the Cook bus line.

Courtesy of Ogden Union Station Collection

■ **TOP RIGHT:** Bamberger Terminal at 24th Street and Lincoln Avenue, circa 1943.

Courtesy of Jason Rusch

■ **RIGHT:** Troops at Ogden Union Station during World War II.

Courtesy of Ogden Union Station Collection 5095

■ **LEFT:** L. P. Hopkins, Southern Pacific superintendent, takes a turn at driving the spike during the 75th anniversary of the Golden Spike, 1944. In the background, left to right: Capt. R. V. Miller, in uniform, of the Naval Supply base; his aide, Lt. Babcock; Gov. Herbert B. Maw, behind and to the right of Hopkins; A. C. Schmidt, Union Pacific; and Everett Michaels of Hyman-Michaels, salvage contractors. *Courtesy of Special Collections Department, Stewart Library, Weber State University*

■ **BELOW:** Employees of the Ogden Union Railroad Depot freight office, circa 1945. Included are Donna Waldram, Lillian Berglund, Linda Leonardi, Mildred Anderson, Audrey Bush, Frances Goff and Norma Taylor. *Courtesy of Donna Staker*

■ **LEFT:** Burton Connery with his son, Buddy, in front of the line shack for the Union Pacific Railroad on 33rd Street and Pacific Avenue, 1943. Burton served as a lineman for the railroad. He also had a band called Bud & His Buddies, which played in the Ogden area. *Courtesy of Daneen Swanke*

■ **FAR LEFT:** Bernice Witten and her son, Lee, looking at cattle in the Ogden Stockyard, 1943. Bernice's uncle, Les Whitlock, helped design and was president of the yard in the 1930s. *Courtesy of Lee Witten*

RIGHT: Union Pacific Roundhouse in Ogden, circa 1945.
Courtesy of Ogden Union Station Collection 5266

BELOW: Terry Roundy, left, and Tommy Hale in front of Terry's father's 1938 Ford in Bonneville Park, circa 1945. *Courtesy of Terry Roundy*

LEFT: Frank Taylor, freight employee at Ogden Union Railroad Depot freight office, 1946. *Courtesy of Donna Staker*

FAR LEFT: Red Caps in front of Union Station, 1946. Included are Leroy Johnson, Roy Goodwin, Johnnie McGhee, Charles Jakes, Elmer Davis, Charles Johnson, George Johnson, William White and William Epps.

Courtesy of Ogden Union Station Collection 4725

FACING PAGE: Browning Chevrolet Co., Washington Boulevard between 26th and 27th streets, circa 1948. Joseph Saam is in the back row, eleventh from the right of the group standing.

Courtesy of Carolyn Saam Bennion

■ **ABOVE:** Bud Favero Utoco service station at the northeast corner of 25th Street and Harrison Boulevard, circa 1955. *Courtesy of Jason Rusch*

■ **BOTTOM RIGHT:** Official car of the Soap-Box Derby, 1948.
Courtesy of Special Collections Department, Stewart Library, Weber State University

■ **ABOVE:** Retirement of engineer Art Corbett, circa 1949. From left to right: Harry Cox, Rod Edens, Art Corbett and John Gibbons. *Courtesy of Ogden Union Station Collection 4707*

■ **Below:** Rosalie Moyes with her family's 1955 Mercury, Plain City, 1956. *Courtesy of Rosalie M. Hurd*

■ **Right:** Rebuilding the 24th Street viaduct across Wall Avenue, looking south, circa 1970. The Union Pacific & Southern Pacific freight station is on the left. *Courtesy of Jason Rusch*

■ **Above:** Engineer A. J. Mulhall and his son, Andy, circa 1955. *Courtesy of Ogden Union Station Collection 4706*

■ **Left:** Locomotive leaving Naval Supply Depot in Clearfield, circa 1955. *Courtesy of Jason Rusch*

33

CHAPTER FOUR

Public Service

When Clearfield Police Chief Herbert Mottishaw retired in 1969, he was given honors and parties throughout the city.

He was praised by the city council. A local high school student, Gary Acevedo, painted a picture for him that was presented at a Christmas party.

And finally, at an assembly of 500 students at Wasatch Elementary School, students presented him with a "gold pen and pencil set and an expensive wallet," according to a *Standard-Examiner* story that ran Dec. 21.

Chief Mottishaw's view of his job was humble. "If more people put their arms around the youth instead of criticizing them, there would be a lot less trouble."

It was a small-town vision of crime prevention, but even though war work in World War II added 57,000 workers to the Top of Utah's payrolls, the area remained a "small town" by most measures.

The work of the war unified both Weber and Davis counties behind one cause, whether it was the Army Air Corps at Hill, the Navy at Clearfield Naval Supply Depot, or the Army at the Utah General Depot. Thousands of families had sons, husbands, daughters and wives serving overseas, so the work was very personal.

That built a community ethic that lasted long after the war ended.

How intimate, and small, things were, is illustrated by Chief Mottishaw's biggest accomplishment in his four-year term:

He implemented, for the first time ever, 24-hour police protection in his town.

■ **Left:** Review of Ogden City Schools R.O.T.C. Exhibition Squad and Band in connection with the premiere of "This Is Your Army," February 1955. Left to right: unidentified military policeman; Adm. George Benerschmidt, United States Navy, Commanding Clearfield Naval Supply Depot; Gen. Herbert A. Hall, Commanding Utah General Depot; Col. Phillip Foote of Hill Air Force Base; and Maj. Robert Fuller, Commanding Ogden Arsenal. *Courtesy of Special Collections Department, Stewart Library, Weber State University*

■ **Right:** The Weber County Sheriff's Posse on the rodeo grounds, 1944. The group was organized circa 1942. *Courtesy of Florence Hunter*

LEFT MIDDLE: First Sgt. Floyd Lawrence Huston served with a railroad company in the Army during World War II in Africa, Italy and France, 1942. *Courtesy of Lois Holmes Huston*

LEFT: Junior Mumford of Ogden served in the Navy, 1942. *Courtesy of Donna Staker*

FACING PAGE: Defense Depot Ogden, circa 1943. Included are Charles McCarthy, far left, and Ed Vendell, behind the counter. *Courtesy of Ogden Union Station Collection*

TOP LEFT: Clearfield Navy Base Fire Station No. 2, 1944. When the navy depot closed, businesspeople bought the buildings in 1963 and made them into the Freeport Center, a bustling manufacturing and distribution center. *Courtesy of Karen K. Stoker*

BELOW: Purchasing and Contracting, Base Procurement of Hill Air Force Base, 1944. First row on the left is unidentified. Starting in the front center and going back: Rosemary Thinnes, unidentified and Ida Batchelor with the rest unidentified. Next row to the right: Irene Haywood, Blanche Rogerson, Shirley Arnold, Ada Weedope, unidentified, Jean Sorenson with the rest unidentified. Right row: unidentified, Yvonne Layton, Dorothea Mueller with the rest unidentified. *Courtesy of Shirley Arnold Hanzelka*

ABOVE: Workers at the Utah General Depot, 1943. Left to right: Lou Molding, Lena Wilson and Thelma Thompson. They worked in a warehouse with German and Italian prisoners of war. *Courtesy of Betty Kap*

■ **ABOVE:** Unloading a Duck, DUKW, at Ogden Arsenal during World War II. Great numbers of these amphibious vehicles were serviced at Ogden Arsenal on their way to overseas battle fronts.
Courtesy of Special Collections Department, Stewart Library, Weber State University

■ **FAR RIGHT:** Mechanical loading equipment saved time and labor at Utah ASF Depot during World War II.
Courtesy of Special Collections Department, Stewart Library, Weber State University

■ **RIGHT:** Jake Van Meeteren at home on leave from the service with his mother and father, Anna and Karel Van Meeteren, 1942.
Courtesy of Jean Van Meeteren

■ **ABOVE:** During World War II, many nurses enlisted and were stationed near military units or in military hospitals, creating a shortage in community hospitals all over the country. A new organization called "Utah State Council of Defense," together with Weber County and Ogden City, instituted a program enlisting women to volunteer to attend a program to learn the skills of a nurse's aide. Donating their free time as part of the war effort, the graduates served as nurses' aides at the local Dee Hospital. Mabel Farr Harris is on the left in the front. Mabel volunteered and received her graduation certificate from the Weber County Defense Council in 1944. She had originally been a teacher, the first special-education teacher in Ogden. She later obtained a civilian position at Hill Air Force Base. During the war, she worked in the section that dispatched parts to repair airplanes. *Courtesy of Wilma S. Smith*

■ **ABOVE RIGHT:** Frank Van Meeteren home on leave from the Navy, 1944. He is with his sisters, Caroline, left, and Nellie. *Courtesy of Jean Van Meeteren*

■ **RIGHT:** Eugene "Bud" VanDeGraaff in Bend, Oregon, 1944. Bud spent his years in the Army training dogs for the service. *Courtesy of Ellen VanDeGraaff Mitchell*

■ **LEFT:** Carl Hodson home on leave from the Army before going to Korea, August 1945. He is with his daughter, Launa, at the Floyd McFarland Sr. home on 12th Street. *Courtesy of Launa Hodson Barrow*

■ **FAR LEFT:** Amie Daniel, age 25, sitting at the cash register during lunch at Hill Air Force Base, 1943. *Courtesy of Daneen Swanke*

39

■ **Facing page:** Summer encampment at Hill Field, 1947. This shows one-quarter of the facilities at the base. It became known as Hill Air Force Base in 1948 following the detachment of the Air Force from the Army Air Corps. *Courtesy of Jason Rusch*

■ **Below:** First police car in Clearfield, 1947.
Courtesy of Norma Zampedri

■ **Bottom right:** Navy Base Fire Department, Clearfield, 1946. *Courtesy of Karen K. Stoker*

■ **Middle:** Lynn C. Hartley was a lieutenant in the United States Army Air Corps circa 1943. He served in North Africa and piloted cargo planes. He later worked at Hill Air Force Base.
Courtesy of Doug and Erma Wilson

■ **Above:** Capt. Jacob Earl "Shorty" Manch, Feb. 17, 1947. Shorty was six feet, seven inches tall and was the chief test pilot at Hill Air Force Base. *Courtesy of Daneen Swanke*

■ **Bottom left:** Ogden police officer Clarence M. Bean joined the department in March 1944. He received injuries in the line of duty that eventually took his life, May 1, 1945. His name is on the memorial monument in City Park as one of the officers who lost his life in the line of duty. He was 41 years old and left behind a wife and three children. *Courtesy of Marilyn B. Hansen*

■ **ABOVE:** Ogden Police Department in front of the Municipal Building, circa 1948. *Courtesy of Stephen Foulger*

BELOW: Alpha George Padgett, Chief of Police, Clearfield, 1947. In 1945 he was appointed a night watchman. He used his own car to check the doors of local businesses and patrol the city. He must have done a good job because, in 1947, the city purchased its first police car and appointed him Chief of Police. In his twenty years in that role, he saw Clearfield grow to a population of 10,000, necessitating a force of nine officers. *Courtesy of Norma Zampedri*

ABOVE: Personnel of Flight Test Section of the Maintenance Division at Hill Air Force Base, June 17, 1949. Donald P. Foutz is tenth from the left in the second row. Last names of personnel in the front row, left to right: LeFevre, Killian, Yates, Strand, Johnson, Nomura, Frew, Favero, Redmond and Dellenback. Second row: Pullum, Hayes, Clay, Bott, Grover, Foust, Olson, Peterson, Stauffer, Foutz, Fowers, Glover, Radcliffe, Dusenberry and Terry. Third row: Adams, Bauer, Leland, Harbertson, Acker, Eytcheson, Rives, Cahoon, Charbonneau, Barber, Allsop, Evans, Rieman, Ellis, Doxey, Utzman, Rollins, Hale, Burr, Crompton, Ayre, Bybee and Sugihara. Back row: Noorda, Olsen, Coombs, DeBernard, Lynch, White, Robinson, Carter, Bingham, Mortenson, Burnett, Paul, Wayment, Barben, Stephens, Andrus and Chappell. *Courtesy of David B. Foutz*

RIGHT: Ogden Garbage Disposal Department at work, circa 1948. *Courtesy of Jason Rusch*

FAR RIGHT: Ogden Fire Station No. 1 under construction, 330 26th St., October 1949. *Courtesy of Jason Rusch*

■ **Above:** James Allen, Mayor Harman Peery and Paul B. Hancock in Lorin Farr Park discussing plans for Western Riding Clubs Association activity, April 1946. Paul B. Hancock and his brother-in-law, Lamar Tullis, were the original organizers of the Weber County Sheriff's Posse. James Allen was one of the original members. *Courtesy of Paul Tex and Lynnette Hancock*

■ **ABOVE:** Federal Building on 24th Street and Grant Avenue, circa 1953. *Courtesy of Jason Rusch*

■ **BELOW RIGHT:** Ogden City Council touring the Utah General Depot, March 11, 1952.
Courtesy of Special Collections Department, Stewart Library, Weber State University

■ **ABOVE:** Deputy sheriffs for Weber County, circa 1952, left to right: Raymond Jones, Don Berrett, Blaine Farr and unidentified. *Courtesy of Jeannine Farr*

■ **RIGHT:** First two mayors of South Ogden, H. Guy Child, left, and John M. Reese.
Courtesy of Jason Rusch

45

LEFT: Machinists who repaired landing gear at Hill Air Force Base, 1955. Fred Arthur Arnold is in the front on the left. *Courtesy of Shirley Arnold Hanzelka*

BELOW: Awards presented to the Defense Depot Ogden workers for improvements in the jogger or paper stacker for printing presses and power folding machines, Nov. 19, 1953. With their awards, left to right: George Anderson, W. Vern Harrop and Donald C. Ellis. On the right is Philo T. Ellsworth, Chief, Defense Printing Service. *Courtesy of Lowell Marriott Harrop*

BOTTOM LEFT: Employees of the Airplane Supply Parts Division at Hill Air Force Base looking at the article in the Hilltop Times about the award they won honoring them as the Outstanding Unit for the Month, August 1952. *Courtesy of Wilma S. Smith*

46

■ **RIGHT:** Grant E. Hansen as he was inducted into Army basic training at Camp Roberts, California, 1951. He was selected for Central Intelligence Center schooling in Baltimore, Maryland, and served in Japan and Korea, specializing in psychological warfare. He volunteered to do the tour in Korea in another man's place when he heard the other man would not be able to go home to see his new child. *Courtesy of Marilyn B. Hansen*

■ **ABOVE:** Clarence "Tobe" Johnston, Posse Chief, beside the Hooper School, 1954. *Courtesy of Daleen Johnston*

■ **TOP RIGHT:** Utah Gov. George Dewey Clyde speaking in Ogden prior to the demolition of the historic Broom Hotel, July 8, 1958. *Courtesy of Jason Rusch*

■ **RIGHT:** Louis "Dewey" Leonardi home on furlough from the Korean War, 1953. His family lived at 1781 Gibson Ave. *Courtesy of Rex Leonardi*

■ **ABOVE:** First memorial service at the new monument to Ogden police officers who lost their lives in the line of duty, May 15, 1962. The widows of two officers, Mrs. Hoyt Gates, left, and Mrs. Clarence Bean are placing a wreath on the front of the marker. *Courtesy of Marilyn B. Hansen*

■ **ABOVE:** Postal workers Alfred Larsen and Jack Robinson inside the Ogden Post Office, October 1961. *Courtesy of Ogden Union Station Collection*

■ **TOP RIGHT:** Motorcycle escort for the funeral of Sgt. "Doc" Marshall White, a policeman killed in the line of duty in a gun battle, Oct. 18, 1963. Officers, left to right: Ben Neff, David Reed, Sgt. Ed Hymas, Gene White and Capt. A. W. Foulger. *Courtesy of Stephen Foulger*

■ **RIGHT:** Officer A. W. Foulger with his police car, showing off Ogden's new radar equipment, circa 1955. *Courtesy of Stephen Foulger*

■ **BELOW:** John S. Dye was first mayor of Uintah and served for 20 years. He was born in 1893 and died in 1971. *Courtesy of T. Neil Dy*

■ **BELOW:** Mont Holmes with his son, Craig, in a Weber County Mosquito Abatement truck, 1960. *Courtesy of Lois Holmes Huston*

■ **ABOVE:** Construction of the new Federal Building at 324 25th St., Jan. 6, 1964.
Courtesy of Jason Rusch

■ **RIGHT:** Retirement party for Mable Farr Harris Decker, March 1964. Mable began her career at Hill Air Force Base in June 1942 as a property and supply clerk. Following that, she worked F-89LGM-30 Minute Man Divisions. At the time of her retirement, she was employed as a supervisor supply commodity management officer in the Minute Man Division. Front row, left to right: Edna Wheeler, Lela Stephens, Janette Spencer, Dora Decker, Lana Marlock, Romona Purcell, Jeptha Christensen, Dwight Brush, Lt. Overlee, Mabel Hecker, Verl Lloyd, Robert Harrington, Alma Kilpack and Mr. Lewis. Back row: Robert Wixom, Theron Wood, Rhoda Reynolds, Alan Blain, Gordon Bigalow, Kennard Bybee, Martha Noblih, Anna Wilde, George Hulme, Lillian Askerooth, Junior Varney, Wiliam Wright, Earl Jones, Edward Wardian, Gertrude Giessler, George Christensen, Mary Reed, Ruth Rhead, James Mclaren and Isabell Talarezyk. *Courtesy of Wilma S. Smith*

■ **Right:** U.S. Postmaster General John A. Gronovske, left, and Ed Vendell, Postmaster of Ogden, in the Ogden Post Office sorting room, April 24, 1964.

Courtesy of Ogden Union Station Collection

■ **Below:** Carnegie Free Library on the southwest corner of the Municipal Block, circa 1965.

Courtesy of Leslie Cole

■ **Above:** Employees of Defense Depot Ogden lined up for a presentation, circa 1962.

Courtesy of Dolores Broadbent Longfellow

■ **Left:** Gerald H. Wayment at a crime scene using the new mobile C.S.I., which was one of the first in the state, 1965.

Courtesy of Gary Wayment

■ **ABOVE:** Capt. A. W. Foulger, traffic commander, on the right, in a Pioneer Days Parade, circa 1970. The other rider is unidentified. *Courtesy of Stephen Foulger*

■ **TOP RIGHT:** Dee Memorial Hospital between 24th and 15th streets at Harrison Boulevard, circa 1968. *Courtesy of Leslie Cole*

■ **ABOVE:** Ogden Juvenile Court Staff, December 1966. Front row, left to right: Rose Olesen, clerk; Fred Ziegler, judge; Joe Tite, director of probation; and Willard Call, court baliff. Second row: Trisha Hurley, deputy clerk; Carmer Parker, deputy clerk; Karen Robertson, deputy clerk; Nancy Hori, deputy clerk; Barbara Oliver, college help; Marilyn Dale, probation officer; Evonne Hille, deputy clerk; Carol Morris, college help; and Valerie Larsen, college help. Back row: Horace Carlson, probation officer; Sharon Bevan, probation officer; Marcella Peterson, probation officer; Madie Bott, deputy clerk; Gene McDaniels, probation officer; Armstrong Owens, probation officer; C. Morgan Bosworth, probation officer; and Mike Strebel, probation officer. *Courtesy of Nancy Hori*

■ **LEFT:** Ric Daniel with his two nieces, Lesley and Daneen Connery, shortly before leaving Washington Terrace to serve in the Navy, 1966. *Courtesy of Daneen Swanke*

CENTENNIAL
1842 - 1942

CHAPTER FIVE

Organizations & Religion

To see how important civic and religious organizations were to community life in the Top of Utah in the 1950s, look at a random copy of the *Davis County Clipper*, a weekly paper specializing in community news.

On April 5, 1957 we find:

• The South Davis Lady Lions Club is completing plans for an annual spring luncheon and fashion show.

• The Bountiful Rotary Club announces its annual spring musical and variety show at Bountiful High School.

• The South Davis County Daughters of Utah Pioneers announced an extensive schedule of 15 meetings of camps around the county.

• St. Olaf's Catholic Church Altar Society is meeting to select new officers.

• Priests and teachers of the Farmington First Ward, Church of Jesus Christ of Latter-day Saints, are holding a dance and potluck supper.

• The Farmington First Ward girls' basketball team is winning.

■ **LEFT:** Relief Society Centennial Celebration at the Ogden Tabernacle, 1942.
Courtesy of Special Collections Department, Stewart Library, Weber State University

■ **RIGHT:** Weber County Young Democratic Women's brunch committee, October 1940. Seated, left to right: Helen Stevenson, Elizabeth A. Vance and Margaret Wright. Standing: Harriet Campbell, Dolly Polidor, Ruth Hancock, Katherine McCool and Mary Raleigh. *Courtesy of Special Collections Department, Stewart Library, Weber State University*

• R. W. Brown is giving his missionary farewell at the Bountiful Seventh Ward Chapel.

• The Bountiful Junior Chamber of Commerce is holding its annual cleanup campaign.

Those are just some activities, from one day in one year.

Throughout the Top of Utah, church groups and civic organizations sponsored Boy Scouts, held recitals, organized charity work.

They were many groups doing many things. Looked at from afar, they made up, and held together, one community.

■ **Below:** Members of LDS Weber Stake with their displays of handiwork, May 1942. Orpha Alberts is standing third from the left. *Courtesy of Betty Kap*

■ **Above:** Camp R, Daughters of Utah Pioneers, at their Christmas party at Cobble Cottage, 12th Street and Jefferson Avenue, 1942. Seated left to right: Julia Drake Farr, Ida Marriott Creamer, Ida Farley Ferrin, Margaret Stalle Barker, Violet Norton, Annis Shaw Badger, Mary Farley Marriott, Margaret Worley Sanford, Julia Pauline Shaw Garr, Edith Morris, Leontine Barker Knighton and Bertha Farley Luddington. Standing: Adelaide "Addie" Ward Shaw, Arta Blakely, Rose Sawyer Chase, Harriet Jones Read, Mamie Newman Stone, Maude Wilson, Mary Wilson Issacson, Isabel Chase Jones, LaPreel Eyre, Lily Barker Richards, Laura Tribe, Jennie Herbert, Jennie Farr Budge and Viola Read Badger. *Courtesy of Jerry Harrop*

■ **Left:** Ogden All-Girls' Orchestra, Ben Lomond Hotel Ballroom, April 6, 1941. The orchestra of women was formed during wartime as the men were serving in the Armed Forces. Front row, left to right: Viola Bennett, unidentified, Ida Marriott, Marjorie McKee, unidentified, Beverly Jergens, unidentified, Kathryn Piper and Barbara Taylor. Second row: Verdene Webb, Marjorie Nelson, unidentified, Nell Barnett, Natalie Cox and Betty Peterson. Back row: LuElla McPherson, unidentified, Donna Denkers, Fae Seager Hansen, unidentified, Helen Woodbury, unidentified, unidentified, Shirley Chamberlain and Berniece Pettigrew. *Courtesy of Jerry Harrop and Lowell Marriott Harrop*

■ **Above:** Boy Scouts, Ogden 19th Ward, heading out on a camping trip, 1951. *Courtesy of Daneen Swanke*

■ **Below:** Weber County Young Democratic Women's Chorus, 1940. Front row, left to right: Dorothy Campbell, Blanche Rassmussen, Erma Wheeler, Marjorie Dew, Louise Coffman, Harriet Campbell, Virginia Holt, pianist Florence Jeffs and director J. Paul Monson. Second row: Ana Boam, Helen Somerville, Dallas Campbell, Frances Gibbons, Bella Buswell, Blanche Margerber, LaVon Averette, Stella Beveridge, Irma Langford, Elizabeth A. Vance and Gladys Jugler. Third row: Dorothy Boam, Emma Lou Kammeyer, Grace Tanner, Marie Fife, May Jugler, Edwina Knapp, Toni Child, Helen Stevenson, Norma Green, Francis Parry, Ila Hill, Francis Davis, Madge Watts, Ruth Samuelson and Donna Adams.

Courtesy of Special Collections Department, Stewart Library, Weber State University

■ **Above:** Ogden LDS 12th Ward, Relief Society presidency and board, Feb. 3, 1947. Ida Farley Ferrin, president, is seated in the center. *Courtesy of Lowell Marriott Harrop*

■ **Top right:** Indian Student Placement Program sponsored by The Church of Jesus Christ of Latter-day Saints, 1951. Standing, left to right: Gerald Dearden, Alice Wanika, Zana Arizana and Wilma Dearden. Kneeling is Jimmie Slater. *Courtesy of Dixie Holmes*

■ **ABOVE:** Young members of the Ogden Exchange Club entertained by Gene Autry at Hotel Ben Lomond, July 1947. Autry told the kids the highlights of movie-making, signed their autograph books and sang for them. Kent Pantone is immediately to the right of Gene Autry. *Courtesy of Sharon Pantone and Jean Sutherland*

RIGHT: Clearfield LDS 2nd and 4th Ward singing chorus, 1947. *Courtesy of Karen K. Stoker*

BELOW: Scout Troop No. 47, LDS 19th Ward, Weber Stake, 1943. Front row, left to right: assistant scout leader Cyril Stanger, Robert Williamson, Wayne Stanger, Jimmy Scadden, Donald Griffith and scout leader Maylin Call. Second row: Robert Dodge, Robert Barker, Robert Kempster, Richard Heninger, unidentified and Paul Donaldson. Third row: Jay Cherry, Boyd Varney, Clark Doxey, Jimmy Bond, unidentified and Dee Barker. Back row: Leland Smith, Kenneth Gale, Ray Pincock, Rex Green, Don Kap and Denny Weaver. *Courtesy of Betty Kap*

BELOW: Church dance at Weber North Stake, circa 1952. First row, left to right: Joyce Farr, unidentified, Marilyn Green and Donna Mae Anderson. Second row: Helen Wayment, Coral Decker, Jelean Skeen and Lora Lee Green. Back row: Barbara Blanch, Carolyn Thompson and Jeannine Thompson. *Courtesy of Jeannine Farr*

■ **Right:** Boy Scout Troop 30 accompanied LDS President David O. McKay and his entourage on a ride to La Plata in 1957. *Courtesy of Doug and Erma Wilson*

■ **Above:** Sons of the Utah pioneers invited LDS President David O. McKay, front and center, for a ride to La Plata, a mining ghost town, in 1957. McKay delivered the mail and the newspaper to La Plata in his youth. *Courtesy of Doug and Erma Wilson*

■ **Right:** Singing Mothers singing at the Ogden Tabernacle, Sept. 20, 1953. Zesta Geizler conducted the choir. *Courtesy of Jean Sutherland*

■ **Top left:** Ogden LDS 7th Ward Meetinghouse, 13th Street and Adams Avenue. At the dedication ceremony on Feb. 14, 1914, President Joseph F. Smith, leader of The Church of Jesus Christ of Latter-day Saints, "expressed surprise and delight" at the beautiful new building and stated it was the best church building for its size that he had seen. The chapel had stained glass windows donated by the members of the congregation. The building was in use from 1914 to the 1960s. *Courtesy of Jerry Harrop and Lowell Marriott Harrop*

■ **Top right:** Ogden Tabernacle, circa 1958. *Courtesy of Leslie Cole*

■ **Left:** Relief Society building in Huntsville, circa 1960. It was built by LDS women to provide services to anyone who needed assistance. The women helped raise money by walking down Ogden Canyon selling eggs and assisted with the digging and building of the facility. *Courtesy of Doug and Erma Wilson*

■ **Far left:** Boy Scout Troop 12, 1956, was sponsored by the Ogden LDS 7th Ward. Sitting in front, left to right: Don Atkinson, Jay Macfarlane, Lyndon Price and Dennis Wirick. Kneeling: Stan LeSeure, Robert Bennett and Richard Slater. Standing: Wells Stephensen, Jerry Harrop, Blaine Glanville, and Scoutmaster Morrill Lofgreen. *Courtesy of Lowell Marriott Harrop*

■ **Above:** 4-H group, circa 1961. Left to right: Shirley Hunt, Sharon Wangsgard, Linda Bronson, Carma Peterson, Kathleen Wood, Kathy Layton, Brenda Frazier and Pam Shupe. Their leader was Fawn Bronson. *Courtesy of Doug and Erma Wilson*

■ **Above:** Eagle Lodge Drill Team, 1966. Included are Amie Daniel, Kay Hawkins and Treva D. Connery. *Courtesy of Daneen Swanke*

■ **Right:** The Does, the women's organization of the Elks, circa 1970. Louise Huston is in the front, second from the right. *Courtesy of Lois Holmes Huston*

■ **Below:** Ogden Elks Lodge on Grant Avenue, circa 1960. *Courtesy of Lois Holmes Huston*

■ **BELOW:** Junior Sunday School class during the last meeting at Marriott Meeting House, 1965. *Courtesy of Dixie Holmes*

■ **BOTTOM RIGHT:** Marriott Meeting House prior to being demolished in 1965.

Courtesy of Dixie Holmes

■ **ABOVE:** F.O.E. 2472 Utah State Auxilliary, May 1971 convention. Front row, left to right: Hazel Shattuck, Peggy Lucas, Beverly Spark, Delores McLendon and Beverly Koger. Back row: Mary Slade, Rose Williams, Afton Wienburger, Dorothy Janes, Auda Phelps, Beth Hadlock and Arvilla Chase. *Courtesy of Daneen Swanke*

■ **BOTTOM LEFT:** Primary teachers during the last meeting at Marriott Meeting House, 1965. Front row, left to right: Ruby Tracy, Deola Stevenson, Lila McFarland, Donna Murray and Dixie Holmes. Second row: Pearl Stanger, Nancy Hodson, Adele Lewis, Janet DeVries, Josephine Murray and Julie Kenley. *Courtesy of Dixie Holmes*

CHAPTER SIX

Education

The first black teacher in Utah was Ruby Price, who went to work in the Davis School District in 1950.

She had a very roundabout trip to that job, which she held for 25 years. As with so much that changed about the Top of Utah between 1940 and 1975, blame World War II.

Glen M. Leonard's "A History of Davis County," written for Utah's statehood Centennial, said Ruby and her husband, Ralph, came to Utah in 1942 to work in the rapidly expanding military bases, including Hill Field.

Ralph Price, says Leonard, was the first 20th-century black to settle in Davis County, which in 1940 had a population of just 3,400 people.

"Ralph Price was an army sergeant who oversaw a 250-man construction crew at Hill Field," Leonard writes. "After his discharge, Price brought his wife, Ruby, and their children to Layton, where they purchased a home."

It took Ruby Price two years of applying to get hired by the school district, Leonard writes.

Post-war growth brought more than just the first black teacher. Greek, Hispanic and Japanese immigrants met with resistance, either because of the war or just because they were different.

"Protect us from the transients among us," an established farmer prayed from the pulpit of a North Davis church meeting house in 1944, Leonard says.

But the "transients" of all sorts kept coming — and staying. District enrollment at the end of 1963 was 26,000 students, almost eight times the county's entire population just 23 years before. That number rose to 33,990 in 1970 and has boomed ever since.

■ **LEFT:** Fifth-grade class at Plain City School, 1940. Vera Palmer is the teacher.
Courtesy of Jean Van Meeteren

■ **RIGHT:** Polk School, 1940.
Courtesy of Special Collections Department, Stewart Library, Weber State University

■ **BELOW:** Pingree Elementary School third-grade class, 1942. The school was located on 30th Street. The principal was Don Barney. In the front row, Paul Donaldson is on the left, with the rest unidentified. Middle row, left to right: Charles Smith, John Whetton, Mildred Hipwell, Barbara Brown, Robert Pierson, Shirley Grissinger, unidentified, unidentified, Lou Jean Morley and Martha Ann Crittenden. Back row: Sharon Palmer, Kay Donaldson, Margaret Coop, Kay Wilson, unidentified, unidentified, Betty Wilson, Sally Moore, unidentified and Mary Ann Wise. *Courtesy of Betty Kap*

■ **ABOVE:** Mound Fort Elementary School fifth grade, 1941. Front row, left to right: Lynn Harris, unidentified and John Owens. Second row, unidentified, unidentified, unidentified, Keith Roberts, Harlen Hancock, Mark Allen, Bob Koger, Bernice Lynch, Shirley Morriss, Sharon Anderson and LaMar Facer. Third row: unidentified, Lorraine Chase, Jerrie Chase, Ardith Parkinson, Tom Cook, unidentified, unidentified, George Cawlishaw, Margaret Spendlove and Marilyn Penrod. Back row: Wayne Walker, Charles Eddy, Vernard Smith, Mona Cobb, unidentified, unidentified, Orren Walker, Dale Swenson, Bert Swenson and unidentified. *Courtesy of Dale G. Swenson*

■ **RIGHT:** Mound Fort Elementary School first-grade class taught by Ms. McCracken, April 17, 1941. Marilyn Bean is in the second row, sixth from the right. *Courtesy of Marilyn B. Hansen*

■ **RIGHT:** Weber College, circa 1946. *Courtesy of Leslie Cole*

■ **ABOVE:** Washington Elementary School third-grade class, 1941. Ted Salerno is second from the right in the first row.

Courtesy of Donna Salerno

■ **RIGHT:** First graduating class in the School of Beauty at Weber College, June 29, 1941. Included are Beth Farmer, Peggy Bott, Madeleine Marriott Harrop and Adara Kidman.

Courtesy of Jerry Harrop

■ **ABOVE:** Lorin Farr Elementary School students, 22nd Street and Harrison Boulevard, circa 1942. The front row is unidentified. In the second row, Ruth Beishline is first on the left, Clarene Clifton is third, Annette Greenwell is sixth and Renee DeBry is seventh. Third row: Alta Kendell is fifth; Larry Miller is sixth. Back row: Dolores Broadbent is fourth.

Courtesy of Dolores Broadbent Longfellow

■ **RIGHT:** West Weber School first- and second-graders, 1941. Front row, left to right: Robert Hawkins, Rudy Gerradelo, Clark East, Alan Heslop, Edwin Penman, Larry Charlton and LaVor Hipwell. Second row: Bob Singleton, Sheron Bitton, Larry Handy, Jean Barrows, Carl Shackleford, Sharon Heslop, unidentified, Evelyn Wagstaff and Reed Hancock. Third row: Evelyn Penman, unidentified, Francis Dalpais, Emma Hipwell, Jean Wright, Lou Jean Heslop, Shirley Peterson and Elaine Charlton. Back row: Miss Woods, Mona Ree Blanch, Orlyn Heslop, Don Griffin, Gerald Farr, Leon Heslop, Glen Ray Hogge, Roy White, Robert McLeon and Jean Hadley. *Courtesy of Jeannine Farr*

■ **Top left:** Third-grade class at Mound Fort, 1946–47. Mrs. Hiatt is their teacher. *Courtesy of Jean Sutherland*

■ **Above:** Kindergarten at Dee School, summer 1946. Kindergarten was held a couple of hours a day for six weeks during the summer. In the front row, fifth from the left is Keith Shupe, seventh is Jay Barnett and tenth is Gerry Richardson. In the back row, left to right: Helen (unknown), Joyce Tueller, Eleanor (unknown), unidentified, unidentified, Sharol Wahlen, Carol Evans, Sally Little, Carol Rackham, Sue Harris, Nancy Cole, Jolene Wright, unidentified and Shirley Martin. *Courtesy of Nancy Hori*

■ **Below:** North Davis Junior High flag, 1947. Ida Underwood is on the left. *Courtesy of Karen K. Stoker*

■ **Above:** Mound Fort Junior High School tenth-grade Pep Club, 1943–44. Front row, left to right: Joy Parry, Eva Watkins, Ramona Messerly, Joy Sant, Josephine Pagano, Dotty Jackson, Velma Dingley, Marion Blackinton, Deloris Stuart, advisor June White, Ruth Paulson, Connie Jensen, Betty Lou Widmeyer, Delores Taylor, Doris Batchelor, Kathryn McKinstry, Donna Baker, Ruby Bronson, Gwen Peterson, Edith Shaw and Iris Carroll. Second row: Thelma Betteridge, Lael Eyre, Pauline Poulter, Marilyn Dawson, Shirley Anderson, Carol Anderson, Annette Bruerton, Jacqueline Gibbons, Ruth Crawford, Joyce Hutchinson, Jane Ann Slater, unidentified, Donna Linford, Roma Kidman, Ethel Day, Lucille Nyland, Donna Smith, Ellenjean Ririe and Doris Coy. Third row: LeJeanne Allen, Edris Hewitt, Lorraine Stoddard, Lenore Chase, Louise Ellis, Claire Sanford, Ida Poce, Janice Goodway, Ardis Whitaker, Beth Judd, Shirley Petersen, Audrie Edwards, Joanne Ridges, Orvilla Lash, Sylvia Bobolis, Shirley Hardman, Melba Moore, Carma Swenson, Colleen Wheeler, unidentified and Colleen Jones. Fourth row: Alberteene Hammer, Afton Richards, Cleo Smith, Myrna McLatchie, Renee Smith, Beverly Edson, Iona Harper, Patricia O'Brien, Eleanor Laughter, Maxine Lamborn, Betty Etterlein, Irene Reno, Louise Brewer, Lou Jean Burnett, Jean Henderson, Patsy Allen, Annette Wilson, Shirley Craycroft and Dorothy Wines. Fifth row: Dixie Hansen, Lou Ann Toller, Donna Manning, Marjorie Jones, Geraldine Palmer, Vivian Ahrens, Lucille Burton, Barbara Tellison, Wilma Weaver, Joan Cross, Bonnie Scott, Betty Papworth, Clavell Brown, Naida Lou Russell, Esther Gray, Evelyn Kent, Annabel Martin, Gwen Call, Erma Young and Roberta Carr. *Courtesy of Deloris Stuart Holley*

■ **ABOVE:** Ogden High School R.O.T.C. Band, 1947. Grant Hansen is in the back, second tuba from the left. *Courtesy of Marilyn B. Hansen*

■ **ABOVE:** Pingree Elementary School third-grade class, 1948. Buddy Connery is in the back row on the right. *Courtesy of Daneen Swanke*

■ **BOTTOM LEFT:** Seventh-grade class at Lincoln Elementary, 1947. Miss Randall is the teacher. Marilyn Bean is in the back row, fifth from the left. *Courtesy of Marilyn B. Hansen*

■ **BOTTOM RIGHT:** Weber College students returning from a six-week, 6,500-mile "college on wheels" tour, September 1947. They traveled across the southwestern United States to Mexico City, studying biology, zoology, Spanish and geology. *Courtesy of Jack W. Gibbons*

■ **Above left:** Uintah Elementary School, 1950, first-, second- and third-grade boys. Front row, left to right: unidentified, Neil Bybee, Gordon Pringle and Allen Kendell. Second row: Ted Peterson, Delane Bybee, Neil Dye, Mario Ornelias and Don Nelson. Back row: Gordon Coleman, Earl Hill, Michael Mildon, Sonny Theofault, Stephen Peterson, Clark Bybee, Gary Bybee and Zane Peterson. *Courtesy of T. Neil Dye*

■ **Above right:** Fourth-graders at Polk School, circa 1950. *Courtesy of David Rusch*

■ **Below:** Washington Terrace Elementary School students, 1948. Duane Walters is third from the left in the middle row. The teacher is Mrs. Salmon. *Courtesy of Marilyn Holmes Walters*

■ **Above:** Plain City Elementary School class, 1950. Front row, left to right: Dennis Maw, Jeff East, Kent Hodson, unidentified, Earnest Hansen, Lewis Brown, Carlos Helsop and Leon Taylor. Second row: Maye Endow, Linda Knight, Elaine Rogers, Kay Folkman, Carole Carver, Ilene Bingham, Milo Ross and Brent Platt. Back row: Carolyn Olson, Connie Poulsen, Kay East, Georgia Heggs, Kennneth Clark, Fred Coy, Kenneth Wayment and Joyce Carver. The teacher is Mrs. Jenkins. *Courtesy of Carole Carver Ellis*

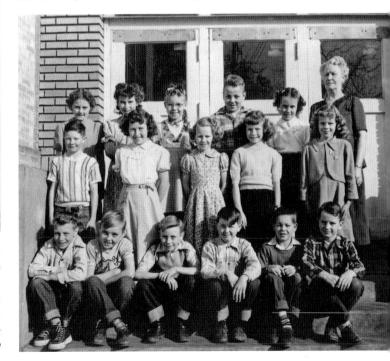

■ **Above:** Pingree Elementary School fifth grade, 1950. Buddy Connery is in the front on the right.
Courtesy of Daneen Swanke

■ **Right:** Plain City Elementary fourth-graders, 1950. Front row, left to right: Ramon Rizzi, Lynn Folkman, Dean Judkins, Bobbie Wayment, Neil Decker and Robert Holbrook. Second row: Kent Hodson, LaRee Wheeler, Connie East, Sherille East and Barbara Jean Robins. Back row: Diane Rogers, Theola James, Carol Anderson, Lynn Taylor, Rosalie Moyes and teacher Bertha Palmer. *Courtesy of Rosalie M. Hurd*

■ **ABOVE:** Burch Creek School classroom, South Ogden, 1951. Rae Chadwick is the teacher. *Courtesy of Paul Tex and Lynnette Hancock*

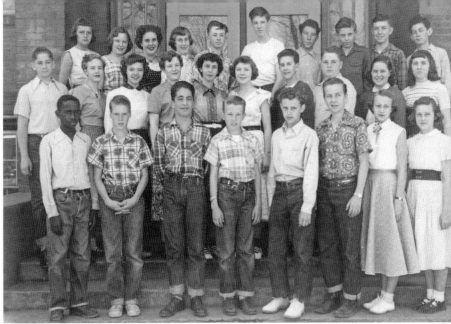

ABOVE: Physical education at Weber High School, 1950. From left to right: Marion Palmer, Nola Moyes, Jean Taylor and Jeannine Thompson. *Courtesy of Jean Van Meeteren*

RIGHT: Wilson School sixth-grade class, 1950. First row, front to back: Ronald Parker, Harry Osborne and Joyce Morrow. Second row: Dennis Craynor, Mary Kay Stanger, Keith Hadley, Jackie Ulibarri, Jimmie Dance and Allan Kap. Third row: Doyle Slater, Michael Henich, Merlyn Judkins, Boyd Mark and Lawrence Andrews. Fourth row: Dixie Lee Dearden, Virginia Kirby, unidentified, Albertine Dean, Beverly Walker and Dorine Price. Fifth row: Helen Burrows, JoAnn Berg, Shirley Ann Bingham, Emma Udink, Barbara Henry and Georgia Elmer. The teacher is Miss Vera Shaw. *Courtesy of Dixie Holmes*

TOP LEFT: Pingree Elementary School, 1951–52. Buddy Connery is the fourth person back in the fourth row. The teacher is Mrs. Pike. *Courtesy of Daneen Swanke*

TOP RIGHT: Lewis Junior High School seventh grade, 1952. *Courtesy of Daneen Swanke*

■ **ABOVE:** Wilson Elementary School fourth-grade class, 1951. Gar Hunter is in the back of the second row of desks. *Courtesy of Florence Hunter*

RIGHT: First-grade class at Lewis School, 1951–52. Val Pantone is fifth from the left in the front row. *Courtesy of Sharon Pantone*

BELOW: "Jolly 17" group from Weber High School, May 1952. In front are Joyce Farr and Jelean Skeen. Second row, left to right: Annette Cook, Marion Rhees, Nola Moyes, Ranae Rhees, Sheron Britton, Alice Maycock and Jeannine Thompson. Third row: Austa Fernelius, Janet Cragun, Sheron Stephens, Loralee Green, Carol Norseth, Marilyn Green, Sally Powell and Donna Anderson. *Courtesy of Jeannine Farr*

RIGHT: Wilson School first-graders, September 1951. Front row, left to right: Ronald Hill, Michael Robinson, unidentified, Rudy Dalla, Brent Hodson, Terry (unknown) and Wayne (unknown). Second row: David Pagano, Margaret Vaughn, Orma Greenwell, Loralee Oleson, Sandra DeYoung, Cherilyn Parker, Linda Thompson, Dixie Stanger and Billy Mark. Third row: Doyle Sexton, Lee Gibson, Ross Hansen, Jean Hodson, Leon Graves, Ray Ellis, unidentified, Lynette Bingham and Connie Wills. The teacher is Ethel Stanford.

Courtesy of Jean Hodson Branch

RIGHT: First-graders at Mound Fort, 1952–53. Larry Huston is on the left in the second row. *Courtesy of Lois Holmes Huston*

BOTTOM RIGHT: Wasatch Elementary School, 1953. Front row, left to right: teacher Sybel Olson, Richie Wadman, Larry Ross, Larry Binns, Richard Speechly, Phillip Patterson, Sam Stock, Jimmy Eastip, Leone (unknown) and Robert Williams. Second row: Barbara Sears, Joan Wingsguard, Linda Kayling, Lynne Mathies, Virginia Richie, Francis Stratford, Beth Keller, Judy Taylor, Ronnie Stevenson and Susan Wigman. Third row: Mike Farr, Clair Baggs, Marilyn Reed, Sandra Taylor, Harold Walcott, Sam Williamson, Craig Evans, Mary Louise Anderson, Sandra West and David Langford. *Courtesy of David Langford*

BELOW: Recess at Mound Fort Elementary School, March 1953. Boys from left to right: Wells Stephensen, Jerry Wilson, Jimmy Chatlin, Jerry Harrop, Dennis Wirick, Jimmy Gardner, Brent Crook and Ralph Allen. *Courtesy of Jerry Harrop*

RIGHT: Boys at recess at Plain City Elementary School, 1951. In back are Lynn Folkman, left, and Robert Holbrook. In front are Neil Decker and Kent Hodson. *Courtesy of Rosalie M. Hurd*

FAR RIGHT: Weber State College building activities on the new site, circa 1955.
Courtesy of Archives, Stewart Library, Weber State University

ABOVE: Third-grade class, Quincy School, 1955–56. Included in the front row: David Hansen, David Storey, Dennis Fowler, Michael Knowles, Guy Hinchcliff, Tommy VanCleave, Richard Gillmore, David Zundel, Ken Hadley, Robert Hillier and teacher Mrs. Stark. Middle row: Judy Young, Elaine Stimpson, Jolene Nalder, Jessa-Lee Rassmussen, Kristy Hanson, Delpha Bingham and Linda Keller. Back row: John William Swanke, Glenna Thomas, Susan Adams, Janet Jensen, Marie Weston, and Roberta Bearve. *Courtesy of Daneen Swanke*

RIGHT: Bonneville Park Elementary School class, circa 1954. Yvonne Roundy is third from the left in the second row; Jimmy Borgono is fourth from the left in the third row. *Courtesy of Terry Roundy*

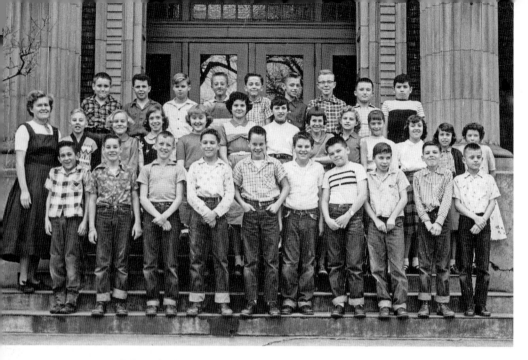

BELOW: Mrs. Sour's kindergarten class at Pingree Elementary, 1955–56. Front row, left to right: unidentified, Herman Palila, Art Martinez, Howard Kennedy, Donny Greenfield, John Carperter and Blaine Breese. Second row: Annette Davis, Susan McCamish, Jann Hales, unidentified, Kathy Kariya, unidentified, Valerie Gilstrap and Donna Atwood. Back row: Mrs. Sour, unidentified, unidentified, Bernice Campbell, Joe Orozco, unidentified, Ronald (unknown), Ben Abeyta, unidentified and Savannah Chess. *Courtesy of Donna Salerno*

ABOVE: Sixth-grade class at Washington Elementary School taught by Mrs. Janet Knowles. In the front row, Billy Story is on the left, David Foutz is fourth and Dale Johnson is sixth. Second row: Mrs. Knowles is on the left with Gary Beech second, Cheryl Morris sixth and Kay Duncan seventh. In the back row, fourth from the left, is Phil Greenwood. *Courtesy of David B. Foutz*

LEFT: Weber High School Warriorettes and marching band, 1956. They are at Municipal Park prior to the Pioneer Days Parade, 1956. The Warriorettes are, front row, left to right: Karen Peterson, Sherry Cottrell and Dixie Lee Dearden. Second row: Ann McGregor, Julianne Barrett and Jolene Hess. Third row: Sharon Cottrell, Leigh Ann Halls and Claudia Simpson. *Courtesy of Dixie Holmes*

BELOW: Graduates of Weber High School, 1960. Launa Hodson is the fifth person in the second row. *Courtesy of Launa Hodson Barrow*

■ **ABOVE:** Lewis Junior High School Concert Band, February 1955. Clarinets: Gerald Peterson, Janet Nixon, Michael Phillips, Michael Moore, Tommy Patterson, Joe Buehler, Janean Yearsley, Joe Jenkins, Stephen Wessler, Lee Whaley and DiAnn McIntire. Cornets: Bobby Hazen, David Clay, David Wanlass, Kent Weir, Charles Hetzel, Joe Wise, Joe Andrus and Don Hebard. Oboe: Karen Davis and Barbara Buss. Violins: Joan Christensen, Joan Moore, Dale Driscoll, Cherie Jensen, Henry Bradbury, Barry Richins, Linda Watson, Kristie Gardner, Cheryl Paxton, Frances Richins, Anita Hall and Phyllis Henson. Violas: Jean Ann Messenger and Beverly Hallet. Cellos: Judy Rae Parke and Louise Carver. Flutes: David Butler, Karen Nichols and Mary Osborn. French horn: Jimmy Arbon, Walter Jay, Tommy Webber, John Ellis and Pat Moore. Trombones: Tony Cluff, Ben Johansen, J. M. Williams, Darrell Jensen and Merrill Willis. Saxophone: Ronald Clay and Reed Baron. Baritone: John Bateman and Narl Allen. The orchestra also included the following instrumentalists. Bass: Carolyn Olson. Percussion: Dennis Thompson and Myron Child. Clarinets: Ernest Shepherd and Charles Rohwer. Bass horn: Michael Burdett, Lee Smith and Steve Jensen. Snare drum: Barry Bingham, Richard Baggs and Lloyd Malan. Bell Lyre: Nancy Cole and Trixie Young. Cymbals: Mark Tillotson. The band director is Loyal West. *Courtesy of Nancy Hori*

■ **ABOVE:** Melodettes from Wahlquist Junior High School, 1955. Front row, left to right: Dian Butt, Ann Cox, Becky Burnett, director Howard Ellis, Rosalie Moyes, Karen Alvord and Carolyn Cobabe. Back row: Gayle Peterson, Linda Maycock, Gwen Gooch, Dyan Wade, Julia Stettler, Patsy Schultz and Jane Valentine.

Courtesy of Rosalie M. Hurd

■ **LEFT:** T. O. Smith Elementary School students, 1956. Larry Huston is in the second row, fourth from the left. *Courtesy of Lois Holmes Huston*

■ **ABOVE:** Weber College building, northeast corner of 25th Street and Adams Avenue, circa 1955. Ogden High and Central Junior High schools were once housed here. *Courtesy of Jason Rusch*

■ **RIGHT:** Horace Mann School sixth-grade class, 1957–58. Larry Huston is third from the left in the second row. *Courtesy of Lois Holmes Huston*

ABOVE: Mound Fort Elementary School, May 1957. Front row, left to right: Marilyn Stallings, Sherry Fields, Barbara Cross, Dianne Hogge, Luana Moulton, Marilyn Streeper, Ruth DeBoer and Jane Richards. Second row: Principal Carruth, Gary Swift, Lynn Jensen, Boyd Price, Jerry Johnson, David Strides, Kenney Miles, unidentified, unidentified and substitute teacher Arlene Hodgson. Back row: Miles Kennington, Lowell Harrop, Glen Curtis, Emanuel Syphers, Craig King, Mark Keller and Steven Edwards. *Courtesy of Lowell Marriott Harrop*

ABOVE: Fourth-grade class from Mound Fort Elementary School, 1958. The front row includes Sherry Fields and the last two on the right are Susan Wirick and Dale Chase. Second row includes Marilyn Stallings, Melanie Howell, Lowell Harrop and Emanuel Syphers. Third row includes June Richards, Diane Hogge and Luana Moulton. Fourth row includes teacher Margaret Sanford and Mile Kennington.

Courtesy of Jerry Harrop and Lowell Marriott Harrop

RIGHT: LaDianaeda Club at Weber College, 1958. Front row, left to right: Shanna Chappell, Frankie Hill, Jane Ann Asay, Sally Lindsey, Judy McFarland, Margaret Miller, Ann Blackinton, Karen Zundell and Layle Combe. Second row: Carolyn Nelson, Barbara Crosby, Kaye Taylor, Nedra Wheeler, Margaret Anderson, Pauline Morley, Gaylene Knight, Narlene Bell, Kathy Nelson, Maridee Upp, Susan Jacobs, Polly Ann Henderson, Gayle Ledingham, Janith Clifton, Marie Russell, Karen McCune, Lynn Marshall and Janice Malouf. Third row: Nancy Roylance, Becky Burnett, Peggy Christensen, Sherri Christofferson, Claudia Ellis, Diane Dursteller, Donna Sparks, Sandra Schofield, LaRee Best, Marlene Harris, Barbara Blanchard, Joan Borger, Elaine West, Geneal Norris, Nancy Cole, Cheryl Ellis and Judy Van Zweden. *Courtesy of Nancy Hori*

■ **ABOVE:** Huntsville School, circa 1960. *Courtesy of Doug and Erma Wilson*

■ **FACING PAGE:** Mount Ogden Junior High band, 1960. David Langford is in the fourth row, sixth from the right. *Courtesy of David Langford*

■ **RIGHT:** Mrs. Goodwin's sixth-grade class at Pingree Elementary, 1961–62. First row, left to right: Cynthia Daniels, Rachel Garcia, Donna Atwood, Lillie Kelley, Judy Patterson, Nanata Taylor, Isabell DeAnda, Arlene Montegon and Roy Leene Brooks. Second row: Henry Sanchez, Dinnis Gill, Edward Trujillo, Tony Long, Jerry Aldous, Tommy Mandez, Richard Pulido and Nicky Villalobos. Third row: Karen Haydon, Lupe Ramos, Kathy Kariya, Sharon Brooks, Robert Harper, Edward Owens, Pat Dilbine, Tommy Noreiga and William Richardson. *Courtesy of Donna Salerno*

■ **ABOVE:** Officers of the Otyokwa social club at Weber College, 1960. From left to right: Norene Howes, Rosalie Moyes, Betty Ballard, Shannon Reyns and adviser Irene Parker. *Courtesy of Rosalie M. Hurd*

■ **LEFT:** Faculty of Taylor School, circa 1960. Margaret Wilson, school secretary, is in front, second from the left. *Courtesy of Doug and Erma Wilson*

■ BELOW: Class at Valley Elementary School, Huntsville, 1964–65. Huntsville had the first public school in the state of Utah. Front row, left to right: Teddie Clark, Jolene Dalton, Cathy Stoker, Judy Campbell, Vivien Stoker, Geniel Calder and Rhonda Montgomery. Second row: Duane Jackson, Roger Meriam, Jessie Southwick, Kevin Garner, Rulon Jones, Rodney Hardy, Frank Shaw and unidentified. Third row: Oneal Wilcox, Kipp Layton, Kurt Wilson, Vaughn Anderson, unidentified, Wade Harris, unidentified, Gary Gould and teacher Leota Allen. *Courtesy of Doug and Erma Wilson*

■ ABOVE: Ben Lomond High School debate team with Gov. Calvin L. Rampton at the Utah Capitol building, 1966. Front row, left to right: Mary Steinlicht, Carol French, Marsha Haacke, Governor Rampton, Kristine Phillips, Randy Dryer and Clark Taylor. Second row: Carol Turley, LaDale Corbridge, Craig Huss and Bruce Wade. Third row: Don Nuttall, Randy Phipps and Steven Groves. Fourth row: Peter Gillins, Brent Glissmeyer, Larry Willis, Joseph Bryner, Lowell Harrop and Marshall Campbell. *Courtesy of Jerry Harrop*

■ BELOW: Weber State College, circa 1965. *Courtesy of Archives, Stewart Library, Weber State University*

■ **ABOVE:** Pioneer Elementary School second-grade class, 1968–69. Mickie Holmes is in the center of the third row, wearing a tan sweater. *Courtesy of Dixie Holmes*

■ **BELOW:** Weber State Singers, 1970. Women, left to right: Beth Grant, LeAnna Florence, Myrleen Shaw, Verla Jean Urie, Miriam Arnell, Nita Maxfield, Sue Hopkin, Mary Lee Memmott, Valene McFarland and Ann Stauffer. Men: Danny Moulton, Paul Jacobsen, LaMar Taylor, Kenny Hansen, Brian Poll, Lowell Harrop, Jim Behling and Andrew Schow. *Courtesy of Jerry Harrop and Lowell Marriott Harrop*

■ **ABOVE:** T. O. Smith School fourth-grade class, 1969–70. Included are Daneen Connery, Larry Bitton, Kent Stelten, Mike Leavitt, Mike Hasteller, Steve Keberictk, Sherre Stevens, Holly Hoskins and Kelly Tallmen. *Courtesy of Daneen Swanke*

CHAPTER SEVEN

Sports & Leisure

Athletics have always been important in the Top of Utah, both on the professional and amateur levels.

Whether it was Japanese baseball leagues in Syracuse, the Ogden Reds professional baseball or the rough-and-tumble of ward baseball and basketball by members of The Church of Jesus Christ of Latter-day Saints, opportunities to do, or watch, athletic competition abounded.

Al Warden, former sports editor at the *Standard-Examiner*, was a major promoter of sports in the area. The Weber County Centennial History, by Richard Sadler and Richard Roberts, says Warden promoted professional football and boxing matches for decades.

One match, at the Ogden Stadium in 1952, was the Rex Layne/ Ezzard Charles heavyweight fight, with Jack Dempsey as referee. Warden also organized the televised fight of Archie Moore and Joey Maxim in 1953.

"Harlem Globetrotters basketball teams and baseball figures such as Babe Ruth, Ty Cobb, Dizzy Dean and Satchel Page visited Ogden at Warden's invitation," the history says.

The Top of Utah was always a big baseball area. After World War II, a number of adult softball leagues were formed. They needed somewhere to play, which is why so many of the parks around Weber County feature baseball diamonds and backstops.

The Ogden Reds and Ogden Dodgers, ancestors of the current Ogden Raptors, were where baseball greats Steve Garvey, Johnny Temple, Bill Buckner, Tom Paciorek, Frank Robinson and future manager Tommy Lasorda got their start.

On the outdoor recreation front, things also were warming up.

One example: In 1940 the Ogden Chamber of Commerce held a contest to name a new ski area up Ogden Canyon.

The winning entry? Snow Basin.

■ **Left:** Washington Junior High School baseball team, 1943. Team members: Sterling Morris, Dale Hufsteller, Bud Gorderud, Wayne Stronberg, Bob Beard, Bob Busico, Bill Fesseler, Glen Weese, Norman Warrner and Deb Rickets. The coach is Bob Smedon. *Courtesy of Robert Busico*

■ **Right:** Bud & His Buddies playing at the Apache Club in Ogden, 1943. Burton "Bud" Connery is on the drums. *Courtesy of Daneen Swanke*

■ **LEFT:** Entertainment for Naval personnel at the Clearfield Naval Supply Depot. *Courtesy of Special Collections Department, Stewart Library, Weber State University*

■ **BELOW:** Bowling league, circa 1942. Aliene Pantone is second from the left. *Courtesy of Sharon Pantone*

■ **LEFT:** Girls playing in the Ogden River at Camp Atoha in Ogden Canyon, July 1942. Among the campers was June W. Stanger, who took the picture. *Courtesy of Jean Sutherland*

■ **FAR LEFT:** Billie Kap, center, skiing with friends at Snow Basin, 1944.

Courtesy of David Langford

■ **RIGHT:** The Chaperones, circa 1945, left to right: Joe Weakley, Richard Barlin, Frederick Brown, David Tucker and Edward Taylor. *Courtesy of Ogden Union Station Collection 2086*

■ **ABOVE:** Ogden Stake basketball team, champions of 1946–47. Front row, left to right: John R. Newey, Dale Grow, Leon McKay, Norman Montgomery, Bryan Renstrom and George Larkin. Back row: coach Edgar Allen, Quinn McKay, Burns Wangsgard, Keith Renstrom, Blaine Harrop, Keith McKay and Marlow Stoker. Alanzo King was on the team but not present for the photograph. *Courtesy of Doug and Erma Wilson*

■ **RIGHT:** Marilyn Holmes fishing with her father, Orville, 1943. *Courtesy of Marilyn Holmes Walters*

■ **FAR RIGHT:** City Park with facilities for checker players, circa 1945. *Courtesy of Special Collections Department, Stewart Library, Weber State University*

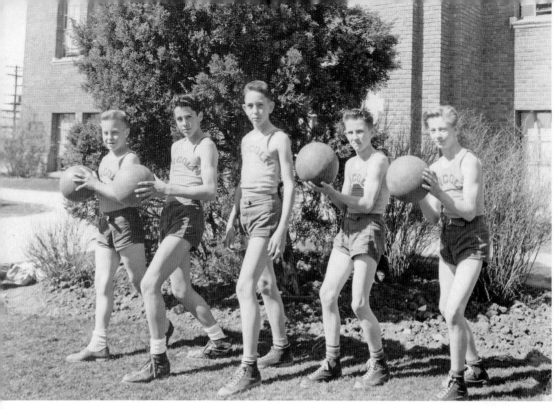

■ **Below:** Mayor Harman Peery, center, hosts the comedy team Abbott and Costello in the Old Mill Restaurant during a war bond drive.

Courtesy of Ogden Union Station Collection 5531

■ **Above:** Lincoln Elementary School basketball team, 1947. Players, left to right: Bill Stitt, Carl Garcia, Russell Whitaker, Rex Fletcher and Don Whitney.

Courtesy of Marilyn B. Hansen

■ **Right:** Anna Belle Weakley at The Old Mill, circa 1942. Anna Belle operated the Porters and Waiters Club on 25th Street.

Courtesy of Ogden Union Station Collection 2091

■ **Far right:** Members of various Utah posses play cowboy polo in West Ogden by the Globe Mills, April 1948. T. J. Morrow is on the left. On the right is Paul B. Hancock who, with his brother-in-law, Lamar Tullis, organized the Weber County Sheriff's Posse in 1942. *Courtesy of Paul Tex and Lynnette Hancock*

RIGHT: Buddy Connery celebrating his ninth birthday in the Ogden River by Lorin Farr Park, 1948. From left to right: Dale Parkinson, Bobby Kapp, Viola Martinez, (unknown) Padilla, Lillis Connery, Janet Nicholson and Buddy Connery. *Courtesy of Daneen Swanke*

ABOVE: Cosmo Club Band, 1947. Left to right: Jimmy Raney, Rasomond Offutt, Ernie Moore and Joe McQueen.

Courtesy of Ogden Union Station Collection 2249

RIGHT: Louis "Dewey" Leonardi, age 16, with his first deer in the Monte Cristo area, October 1947.

Courtesy of Rex Leonardi

FAR RIGHT: Starting point at the Soap-Box Derby, 1948.

Courtesy of Special Collections Department, Stewart Library, Weber State University

■ **Far left:** Larry White with his sled, February 1950. *Courtesy of Betty White*

■ **Left:** Usheretts at Affleck Park, 1952. Left to right: Bobbie Ann Alder, Jeri Scowcraft and Betty Reeder. *Courtesy of Jeri S. Holmes*

■ **Below:** After a successful fishing trip, left to right: Ruth and Jim Fowers, Louis Poulsen and Ralph and Elma Taylor, circa 1949. *Courtesy of Jean Van Meeteren*

■ **Left:** State wrestling champions from Weber High School, 1952. Front row, left to right: Paul Melling, Willis Galvez, Dale C. Johnston, Darrel Hansen, Neil Finders and Harry Papageorge. Second row: coach Mac Tatt, Ivan Anderson, Vernon Miller, Jim Marriot, (unknown) Thompson, Gary Francis, Bert Hulet, Bill Beaver and coach Mel Wood. Co-captains Dale Johnston and Harry Papageorge placed first for the second consecutive year. *Courtesy of Daleen Johnston*

■ **ABOVE:** Ogden Reds baseball team, 1950. *Courtesy of Jeri S. Holmes*

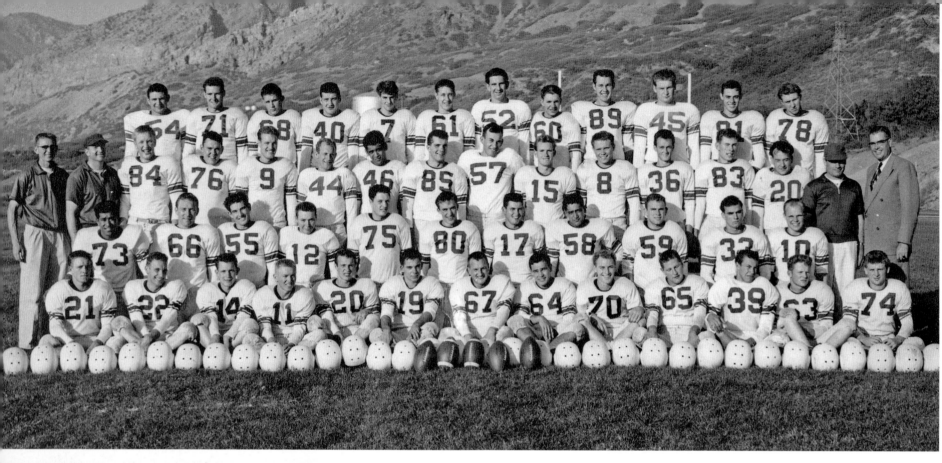

ABOVE: Weber State College football team, 1954. Karl Stoker is in the second row, number 17. College president William P. Miller is at the far right in the second row. *Courtesy of Karen K. Stoker*

LEFT: Marriott Ward basketball team, 1952. Front row, left to right: Frank Slater, Gary Thornock, Larry Thornock, Sherman Willard and Dewey Bingham. Back row: Ronald Greenwell, Jimmy Peer, Gaylen Jensen, C. J. Panter and Gary Dinsdale. They were coached by Leon Carnahan. *Courtesy of Dixie Holmes*

FAR LEFT: Weber High School cheerleaders, 1952. From left to right: Lila Allen, Ranae Draayer, Karen Dayle Read, Lois Standing and Nedra Allen. *Courtesy of Daleen Johnston*

■ **Right:** Lewis Junior High School Pep Club, 1954–55. Front row, left to right: Susan Brown, DeAnn Knudsen, Pat Olsen, Connie Edwards, Carolyn Lambert, Thelma Aldous, Eurika Endo, Janice Malouf, Rosalind Bowman, Linda Malan, Larene Jensen and Neva Lou Taggert. Second row: Janeen Yearsley, Virgie Little, Janis Stewart, Elsie Lopez, Alice Mower, Karen Fife, Susie Scowcroft, Frankie Hill, Gayle Ledingham, Elizabeth Dean, Marlena Harris, Carole Spaun, Linda Clements, Joyce Chess and Gloria Chess. Third row: Yvonne Hock, Judy Bain, Carolyn Pitcher, Gaye Tanner, Carol Stimpson, Karen Davis, Katheleen Tracy, Verlane Richardson, Renee Fife, Marion Howell, Suzy Thomas, Judy Butler, Linda Keep and Vickie Broome. Fourth row: Juanita Guachino, Cheryl Ellis, Emilia Rickter, Marilyn Gilbertsen, Joann Haggstrom, Arlene Thomas, Sheila Shields, Renee Weaver, Betty Austin, Pat Harrington, Julie Huish, Barbara Anda, Anne Van Winkle, Judy Van Zweden, Barbara Ballard, Karen Nichols, Shannon Reyns, Anita Floor and Mrs. Chournos. Cheerleaders in the back row: Judy Degn, Carol Boyle and Nancy Cole. *Courtesy of Nancy Hori*

■ **Above:** Football practice on the Weber High School football field, circa 1953. *Courtesy of Jason Rusch*

■ **Right:** Ogden Reds, Pioneer League champions, 1953. *Courtesy of Jeri S. Holmes*

■ **BELOW:** Lanes at Paramount Bowl, 1961. The business was owned by Maxie Kosof.
Courtesy of Ogden Union Station Collection 1493

■ **ABOVE:** Marriott Ward girls' softball team, division champions, 1959. Front row, left to right: Launa Hodson, Marian Stanger, Dixie Dearden and Marilyn Holmes. Back row: Karen Baird, Sherma Stanger, Mary Kay Stanger, Marilyn Bingham, Sandra Colby and Georgia Elmer. *Courtesy of Marilyn Holmes Walters*

■ **BOTTOM LEFT:** Girls' first year at Camp Beaver, 1951, left to right: Dixie Lee Dearden, Georgia Elmer and Shirley Ann Bingham. *Courtesy of Dixie Holmes*

■ **BOTTOM RIGHT:** Weber High School band forming the big "W" on the football field, fall 1958. The band director is Arch Stokes; the drum major is Phil Mathews; the drum majorette is Lynnette Wolthuis. *Courtesy of Paul Tex and Lynnette Hancock*

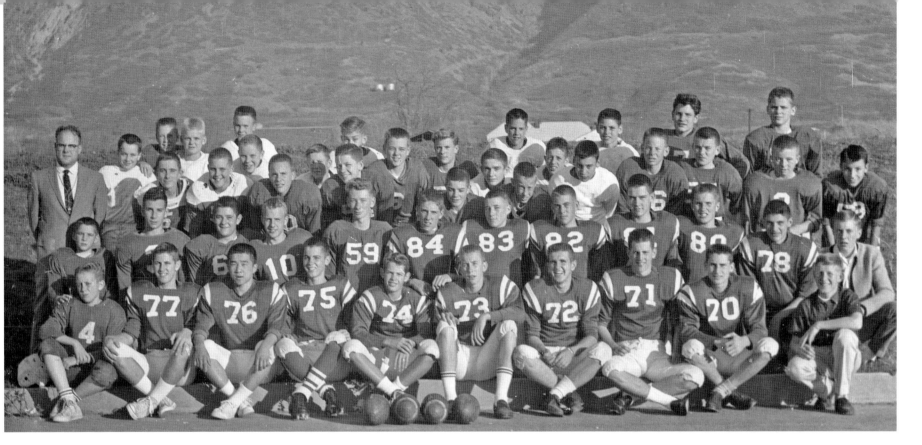

■ **ABOVE:** Mount Ogden football team, 1961. David Langford is in the third row, third from the left. *Courtesy of David Langford*

■ **LEFT:** Mount Ogden Junior High School basketball team, 1961. Front row, left to right: Brent Richins, Scott Larkin, Carl Visser, Ron Blackhurst, Gerald Allen and John Cottom. Back row: principal Mr. Polter, head coach Don Shaw, Terry Monson, Craig Woolley, Greg Thorstensen, Scott Laughton, Paul Neuenschwander, John Webb, David Langford, unidentfied and assistant principal Mr. Carter.

Courtesy of David Langford

■ **LEFT:** Terry Roundy jumping into the outdoor pool at Rainbow Gardens, circa 1958.

Courtesy of Terry Roundy

■ **ABOVE LEFT:** LaHabra 300 Bowl, July 1962. Maxie Kosof is holding the bowling ball.
Courtesy of Ogden Union Station Collection 1497

■ **ABOVE RIGHT:** This slow pitch team from Plain City 2nd LDS Ward took all-church two years in a row, fall 1964. *Courtesy of Florence Hunter*

■ **ABOVE:** Clarence "Tobe" Johnston, left, with his fishing group in Weber County, 1960, left to right: Clarence, Reed Naebit, Mr. Higly, Holy Byee, Mr. Simpson and Thorell Cox. *Courtesy of Daleen Johnston*

■ **RIGHT:** Weber State College baseball team, 1966. They placed fifth in the Big Sky Conference. Front row, left to right: John Zundel, Larry Katol, Harold Prince, Clair Wadman, Ken Caputo and Buddy Brannen. Second row: Larry Pearson, Steve Baglow, Les Mathson, Dick Wilden, Wayne Andreotti, Doug Roundy and Charles Peraset. Third row: coach Dick Williams, Lynn Christensen, John Higgins, Lenny Nielson, Kirk Black, Scott Hansen, Craig Gladwell and pitching coach Ken Hunt. *Courtesy of Archives, Stewart Library, Weber State University*

■ **LEFT:** West Weber church ball team, circa 1972. In front: Carl Hipwell, Lowell Farr and Garth Brown. Back: Andy Heslop, Dale Farr, Ron Surrage, Joe Calderwood and coach Ez Hadley. *Courtesy of Jeannine Farr*

■ **BELOW:** Weber State College baseball team, Big Sky Conference champions, 1970. Front row, left to right: Rourke McDermott, Mike Hall, Glen Paramore, Kelly Hansen, Larry Thorne and Frank Park. Second row: Craig Estell, Barry Bagley, Brad Shields, Larry Cole, Craig Hansen, John Webster, Blake Zimmerman and Stan Buchanan. Third row: assistant coach Fred Thompson, Steve Brophy, Dominic Albano, Kirk Black, Greg Downs, Bob Nicholson, Bill Sowders and coach Blaine Sylvester. Sylvester won Big Sky Conference Coach of the Year that year. *Courtesy of Archives, Stewart Library, Weber State University*

■ **BOTTOM LEFT:** Weber State College basketball players and coach, 1971–72. *Courtesy of Archives, Stewart Library, Weber State University*

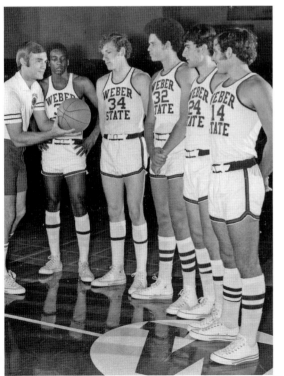

CHAPTER EIGHT

Family & Friends

Dee, Wattis, Lindquist, Marriott, Eccles, Browning and Farr are families that built the Top of Utah.

For example, when the Utah Construction Co. was formed in 1900, it listed, among others, David Eccles.

David Eccles' son, Marriner S. Eccles, founded First Security Bank and became chairman of the Federal Reserve Board.

His closeness to President Roosevelt helped the Top of Utah secure many of the wartime military projects that transformed the area.

The work of those prominent families made it possible for thousands of other families to make livings in Weber and Davis counties. A glance at any local paper from the 1940s and 1950s finds notices of their comings and going.

While Marriner Eccles was hobnobbing with presidents Roosevelt and Truman, for example, the *Davis Clipper* from 1949 reports that Mrs. Milton Call and Mrs. Don DeWitt attended a party at the home of Mr. and Mrs. Vern Thurgood in Syracuse.

The famous and not-so-famous did, however, sometimes meet.

Willie Moore, who ran a barbershop in Ogden's Marion Hotel 50 years ago, and runs one there today, tells of the time in the early 1950s that Eleanor Roosevelt stopped by to visit.

"She told us, 'You guys, don't forget to vote,' " Moore says, "and we told her we wouldn't."

■ **LEFT:** The Van Meeteren family, 1952, lived on 39th Street and Grant Avenue. Front row, left to right: Nellie, Henry, Steve, Anna, Ronnie, Bill and Jennie. Back row: Caroline, Katheryn, Frank, Jake, Carl, Margie and Annie. *Courtesy of Jean Van Meeteren*

■ **RIGHT:** Ronald, Sherman and Lamont Holmes, left to right, at their home on 12th Street, 1940. *Courtesy of Dixie Holmes*

■ **TOP LEFT:** Birthday party for Emma Louise Stoker at her home in Clearfield, summer 1940. *Courtesy of Karen K. Stoker*

■ **TOP MIDDLE:** Mont and Sherm Holmes heading off to school with their lunch buckets, circa 1940. *Courtesy of Lois Holmes Huston*

■ **TOP RIGHT:** Carol Taylor riding her bike in Plain City, circa 1941. *Courtesy of Jean Van Meeteren*

■ **RIGHT:** Mont Holmes, center, playing London Bridge at his birthday party at the Holmes residence, 1941. His brother Ron is on the far left. *Courtesy of Lois Holmes Huston*

■ **LEFT:** Marilyn Holmes pumping water at her family's home in Marriott, 1943. *Courtesy of Marilyn Holmes Walters*

■ **LEFT MIDDLE:** Four-year-old Ronald Holmes with his cow Bossie, 1941. *Courtesy of Dixie Holmes*

■ **FAR LEFT:** Family campout in South Fork, 1940. From left to right: Dennis Craynor, Marilynn Dearden and Dixie Lee Dearden. *Courtesy of Dixie Holmes*

RIGHT: Archibald Stanger with grandchildren Mont, Ron, Sherm and Marilyn after a fishing trip, 1942. *Courtesy of Marilyn Holmes Walters*

BELOW: John F. Gibbons reading the *Standard-Examiner* at his home at 2874 Madison Ave., circa 1940. *Courtesy of Jack W. Gibbons*

ABOVE: Left to right in the front: Jay Nance and cousin Gary Aquino. Back row: Louella and Joyce Nance. *Courtesy of Louella Craig*

BOTTOM RIGHT: Gary Aquino, Jay Nance, Joyce Nance and Louella Nance at the airport, 1941. *Courtesy of Louella Craig*

BOTTOM MIDDLE: Ronald Holmes, circa 1940. *Courtesy of Dixie Holmes*

BOTTOM LEFT: Big sister Jean Ann Stanger with sister Sherry on the left and Richard Stallings, a neighbor, on the right, 437 Cross St., summer 1941. *Courtesy of Jean Sutherland*

■ **Above:** The Padgett family, 1941. *Courtesy of Norma Zampedri*

■ **Right:** Louella Nance, Kaysville, with her cat and Tippy the dog, 1941. *Courtesy of Louella Craig*

■ **Bottom left:** The Ruth Gale family, 3153 Wall Ave., 1942. In front is Clarence, holding onto Kent Rohmer. In back: family friend Bev Evans, Ruth and Lavon Gale. *Courtesy of Bonnie Carrel*

■ **Above:** Mont, Sherm and Ron Holmes with their rifles, July 1942. *Courtesy of Lois Holmes Huston*

■ **Below:** Ralph Taylor with his horse, Pal, and his wife and daughter, Elma and Jean, in the back, 1942. Ralph was the first marshal of Plain City. *Courtesy of Jean Van Meeteren*

■ **ABOVE:** Val Taylor, Brent Taylor, Ralph Taylor, Jean Taylor, Carol Taylor and Karole Maw on horseback in Plain City, circa 1945. *Courtesy of Jean Van Meeteren*

■ **ABOVE RIGHT:** The VanDeGraaff family, 3258 Fowler Ave., June 1943. In front, left to right: John Jr., Fred, Merrill, Luciele and Sherma. Back row: Nell holding Kent, Ellen, June, John, Bud and Wayne. *Courtesy of Ellen VanDeGraaff Mitchell*

■ **LEFT:** Wading in the stream, 1944, left to right: Mont Holmes, Sherm Holmes, Marilyn Holmes, Sharon Stanger and Ron Holmes. *Courtesy of Lois Holmes Huston*

■ **ABOVE MIDDLE:** Launa Hodson on her first horseback ride with her uncle, Grant Hodson, 995 W. 12th St. in Marriott, circa 1944. *Courtesy of Launa Hodson Barrow*

■ **ABOVE RIGHT:** Harold and Norma Rohmer, 1943. He was home on leave from the Army. *Courtesy of Gayle Rohmer Hamer*

■ **Right:** Hooper kids playing at Lea Johnston's home, circa 1940. Blair Johnston is on the left. *Courtesy of Daleen Johnston*

■ **Far right:** Cyril "Cy" Hartley worked for Mountain Fuel Supply, circa 1945. He worked for the company for 43 years. *Courtesy of Doug and Erma Wilson*

■ **Below:** The Daniel family at their home at F4 Navy Way, Washington Heights, 1946. From left to right: Gary, Lester, Amie, Treva, Bill and Nolan Daniel. The woman on the right is Edith Corry. *Courtesy of Daneen Swanke*

■ **Bottom right:** Marion and David Folland waiting for Santa, circa 1945. *Courtesy of Karen K. Stoker*

■ **Bottom middle:** Margaret Schwab Wilson and Wilford "Wiff" Wilson, 1663 Capital St., circa 1944. Wilford worked for the Ogden Union Railway Depot and Margaret was a school secretary. They also owned a greenhouse and floral business. *Courtesy of Doug and Erma Wilson*

■ **Above:** Louise and Carl Hodson with children Launa and Brent. They posed for this photograph right before he was sent to Korea, 1945.

Courtesy of Launa Hodson Barrow

RIGHT: Friends Mary Hokinson and Lillis Connery right before leaving on a camping trip, August 1949.
Courtesy of Daneen Swanke

ABOVE: Jack W. Gibbons and Ray Geiger at the mouth of Ogden Canyon on horses rented from a stable, summer 1946. *Courtesy of Jack W. Gibbons*

BELOW: Eugene Stanger with his daughters, Sheri and Jean, 1946. They were on an Easter picnic near Bear's Cave.
Courtesy of Jean Sutherland

LEFT: Gene and June Stanger's extended family and friends celebrating Easter in Ogden Canyon, 1946. *Courtesy of Jean Sutherland*

RIGHT: Billie Kap with her daughter, Jackie, in a military housing unit in Washington Terrace, 1947.

Courtesy of David Langford

BELOW: John VanDeGraaff with some of his children by his Paramount Dairy delivery truck, circa 1947. In front is John Jr. From left to right: Luciele, John holding Fred, Sherma holding Kent, and Merrill. *Courtesy of Ellen VanDeGraaff Mitchell*

ABOVE FAR RIGHT: Jack W. Gibbons and Betty McGary at Snow Basin, March 8, 1947. They went on to marry on April 21, 1950. *Courtesy of Jack W. Gibbons*

RIGHT: Sliding on Cross Street above Washington Boulevard, January 1946. From front to back: Jean Stanger, Sheri Stanger, Joyce Maddock and Beth Stallings. *Courtesy of Jean Sutherland*

BELOW: Lorenzo Heninger home at 3020 Wall Ave., winter of 1948–49. *Courtesy of Betty Kap*

ABOVE: Madeleine Marriott Harrop, 2nd Class Petty Officer Vern Harrop and their son, Jerry Harrop, 1945.

Courtesy of Lowell Marriott Harrop

BELOW: Col. Graves B. McGary with his wife, Florence, and daughter, Betty Jane, 1948. They lived at 1445 Binford St. Col. McGary retired as Commander of the Utah General Distribution Depot in June 1948. *Courtesy of Jack W. Gibbons*

ABOVE: Cousins Treva Daniel, age six, and Trenna Atchley, age eight, on the step of the Lester and Amy Daniel home at F4 Navy Way, Washington Heights, 1946. *Courtesy of Daneen Swanke*

LEFT: Friends, bottom to top: Karole Maw, Jean Taylor, Karen Taylor, Cheryl Robson, Beth Singleton and Jeannine Thompson, circa 1948.
Courtesy of Jean Van Meeteren

BOTTOM MIDDLE: Eva Bean with her daughters, Marjorie, left, and Marilyn, walking down Washington Boulevard in front of Commercial Security Bank on their way to L. R. Samuels, fall 1947. The photograph was taken by "the man on the street." *Courtesy of Marilyn B. Hansen*

RIGHT: Nance family on their farm in Kaysville, 1947. From left to right: Joyce, Lucy, John Jr. and John Sr. Mary is in the front.
Courtesy of Louella Craig

ABOVE: The Malan family of 16 children were all named by the alphabet. Six of the 16 here, front row, left to right: Alexis Bartholomew, Ernest Frances and Gideon Highly. Back row: Lawrence Maxwell, Nahum Oscar and Parley Quince. Lawrence Maxwell Malan was county clerk for 29 years, until 1962, and married more than 1,500 couples. *Courtesy of Jeri S. Holmes*

RIGHT: Larry Huston visiting Santa at Bon Marche, 1951. *Courtesy of Lois Holmes Huston*

BELOW: David Langford and his mother, Lovina, on the carousel at Lorin Farr Park, circa 1949. *Courtesy of David Langford*

ABOVE: After the Ogden Pioneer Days Parade, 1949. Left to right: Elva Craynor, Wilma Dearden and Dixie Lee Dearden, Lead Majorette. They are standing on Washington Boulevard. *Courtesy of Dixie Holmes*

LEFT: Launa Hodson and Douglas DeVries in the "Wedding of the Flowers" operetta presented by the first-, second- and third-grade classes at Wahlquist School in Farr West, 1948. *Courtesy of Launa Hodson Barrow*

FAR LEFT: Alvin and Marie Stoker with grandson Jerry, 1949. *Courtesy of Karen K. Stoker*

■ Below: Douglas Moyes, Plain City, 1951. He is the son of Walter and Della Clark Moyes. *Courtesy of Rosalie M. Hurd*

■ Bottom left: Alvin Stoker harvesting his carrots from the frozen land, January 1950. *Courtesy of Karen K. Stoker*

■ Bottom middle: John William Swanke, son of Stanley and Shirley Smith Swanke, age one, Aug. 18, 1947. The traveling photographer came to town shortly before Pioneer Days each year. *Courtesy of Daneen Swanke*

■ Above: Eight young men who grew up in the same neighborhood, attended school and church together and accepted calls from The Church of Jesus Christ of Latter-day Saints, Ogden 7th Ward, Ben Lomond Stake, 1950. In front, left to right: William Radmall, Southern States; Kenneth Alford, Uraguay; Lawrence Raty, Swiss-Austria; Arthur Budge, Central States. Back row: Neil Larsen, Eastern States; Dale Swenson, Japan; Elmer VanderDoes, Netherland; Frank Lucas, Australia. *Courtesy of Dale G. Swenson*

■ Above: Three-year-old Vicki Lien in the yard of her home at 317 W. Liberty St., Layton, spring 1950. The car is a 1939 Buick four-door sedan. *Courtesy of Vicki Lien Holley*

111

■ **FAR LEFT:** Cousins Reed Holmes and Danny Brown on their rocking horses made by Leila Holmes, 1955. *Courtesy of Lois Holmes Huston*

■ **LEFT:** Brothers Larry and Jim Huston visiting Santa at Bon Marche, 1952. *Courtesy of Lois Holmes Huston*

■ **BOTTOM RIGHT:** Harold Carver driving his tractor with his family around him, 1952. His grandchildren are on his lap, left to right: Scott Sessions, Randy Russell and Mark Sessions. His niece, Joyce Carver, is on the left; his daughter, Carole Carver, on the right. They are on the Carver farm in Plain City. *Courtesy of Carole Carver Ellis*

■ **BOTTOM MIDDLE:** Alvin and Marie Stoker with their daughter, Ruth, and her children, Margaret, Janet and Kathy, on the family farm in Clearfield, 1952. *Courtesy of Karen K. Stoker*

■ **ABOVE:** Marian Stanger, Launa Hodson and Beverly Gabey in front of Marriott Church, circa 1949.

Courtesy of Marilyn Holmes Walters

112

■ **LEFT:** Rick Huston, 1956, on the traveling photographer's pony. *Courtesy of Lois Holmes Huston*

■ **BELOW:** Jeanne Roylance, Mike Rackam, Gordon "Buster" Roylance, Ellen Roylance and Janet Rackham at the Rackham home at 3043 Adams Ave., July 1956.
Courtesy of Ellen VanDeGraaff Mitchell

■ **ABOVE:** Calvin Waters on a new Case grading tractor in South Weber, 1957. He owned and operated an excavating business. *Courtesy of Janet Gardener*

■ **BOTTOM LEFT:** John William Swanke, a member of the Bumble Bees baseball team, June 3, 1958. *Courtesy of Daneen Swanke*

■ **BOTTOM MIDDLE:** Paul Kent Roundy, back, and Don Eldee Roundy on the traveling photographer's pony in Bonneville Park, circa 1955.
Courtesy of Terry Roundy

■ **ABOVE:** Slumber party, 1956. From left to right: Dixie Lee Dearden, Karen Greenwell, Shirley Ann Bingham, Georgia Elmer, Carolean Bingham, Barbara Henry and Jolene Hess. *Courtesy of Dixie Holmes*

■ **FAR LEFT:** Lois Holmes, Marian Stanger and Marilyn Holmes at a freshwater spring near Monte Cristo, 1955. *Courtesy of Lois Holmes Huston*

■ **LEFT:** Larry Huston on the traveling photographer's pony, 1956. *Courtesy of Lois Holmes Huston*

■ **BELOW:** Dr. Wallace Budge was a family doctor who delivered all of these children of the Archibald and Beatrice Holmes Stanger family. He is seated in the second row with the glasses, 1958. Front row, left to right: Fred Mitchell, Randy Brown, Doug Stanger, Sandra Stanger, Lois Holmes, Janet Minor, Reed Holmes holding a picture of Sherm Holmes, Leon Stanger and Kenneth Mitchell. Second row: Mitch Minor, Merlyn Mitchell, Danny Brown, Debra Minor and Jerry Stanger. Third row: Sharon Stanger Turnblom, Dr. Budge, Bea Stanger holding Kent Brown, Arch Stanger, Marion Stanger holding Donny Stanger, Gayle Turnblom and Georgia Mitchell. Back row: Lynn Brown, Steven Brown, Marilyn Holmes, Mont Holmes, Sherrie Stanger, Dallas Stanger, Jean Ann Stanger, Ron Holmes and Joyce Mitchell. *Courtesy of Lois Holmes Huston*

■ **ABOVE:** Frank Van Meeteren, Harry Kent, Carl Van Meeteren and Bill Van Meeteren pheasant hunting in Plain City, 1954. *Courtesy of Jean Van Meeteren*

RIGHT: Growing beards for Pioneer Days, Royal McBee Printing Company, 22nd Street and Wall Avenue, July 1960. Front, left to right: Jack W. Gibbons, Roy Rackham, Chuck Abbot and Marlin Hocking. Back: Virgil Brockbank, Howard Wadman and Bob Gross. *Courtesy of Jack W. Gibbons*

ABOVE: Bonnie Carrel and her children, Jeff, Sue, Craig and Leslie, 1961. They had this photograph taken to send to Bonnie's husband, Maj. Elton J. Carrel, who was serving in Korea at that time. *Courtesy of Bonnie Carrel*

RIGHT: Seven-year-old Donna Atwood with her Christmas bride doll, 115 Patterson St., 1958. *Courtesy of Donna Salerno*

BELOW: Brenda Van Meeteren visiting Santa in the Sears store, 1961. *Courtesy of Jean Van Meeteren*

BOTTOM RIGHT: Lesley Connery's third birthday party, March 1965. From left to right: Tom Nistler, Lesley Connery, Roxann Hawkins, Daneen Connery and Kim Hawkins. Brad Nistler is in front. *Courtesy of Daneen Swanke*

ABOVE: Carl and Louise Hodson family with the Ellis and Mildred Slater family during the last meeting at Marriott Meeting House, 1965. *Courtesy of Dixie Holmes*

LEFT: Lois Holmes with her horse, Cindy, 1959. *Courtesy of Lois Holmes Huston*

BELOW: The Ruth Gale family, 3153 Wall Ave., July 1964. They are gathered in the 19th Ward chapel. Front row, left to right: Carol Rohmer, Tammy Rohmer, Dawnette Gale, Steve Gale, Vern Gale, Brett Rohmer, Elnora Messina, Craig Carrel, Bonnie Carrel, Susan Carrel, Ruth Gale, Norma Rohmer, Debbie Rohmer, Clara Doos, Anne Doos, Clarence Gale, Kevin Gale, Kathy Gale and Karen Gale. Second row: Marla Foulks, Bill Foulks, Verna Gale, Carol Crossley, Moana Gale, Jeff Carrel, Julie Messina, Leslie Carrel, Janice Rohmer, Gayle Rohmer, Susan Rohmer, Janet Rohmer, Paul Doos, Ruth Doos and Arlene Gale. Back row: Rich Crossley, Tony Messina, Harold Rohmer, Jodi Rohmer, Steve Messina, Ted Doos, Jeff Carrel, Kent Rohmer, Gary Rohmer and David Doos.

Courtesy of Bonnie Carrel

■ **Above:** Quilting bee at the home of Beatrice Stanger, 1968. Left to right: Leila Holmes, Beatrice Stanger, Elaine Horton, Evelean Brown, Joyce Johnson, Ellen Jenkins, Drucilla McFarland, Ruth White, Connie Brown and Denise Forte. Facing the quilt are Rosemary Schoppe, Jessine Pack and Lenore Holmes. *Courtesy of Lois Holmes Huston*

■ **Above right:** Orville Holmes with his horses, Cindy and Penny, in the pasture at home in Marriott, 1961. *Courtesy of Lois Holmes Huston*

■ **Right:** Ruth Macfarlane Gale, 1974, ready to celebrate her 80th birthday. *Courtesy of Bonnie Carrel*

■ **Left:** Kent and Karen VanDeGraaff family, 1974. Kent is holding Arie with Ryan between his knees. Kyle is next to his mom, with Eric in front.
Courtesy of Ellen VanDeGraaff Mitchell

■ **Far left:** Birthday party for Mickie Holmes, 1967, at the Holmes house, 1900 West in Marriott. From left to right: Terrie Hodson, David DeVries, Doug Worthen, Debbie Carnahan, Peggy Stevenson, Mickie Holmes, Debbie Thompson and Ned Greenwell.

Courtesy of Dixie Holmes

CHAPTER NINE

Community

Top of Utah residents are always getting together for something. Whether for parades, musicals, concerts or whatever, they turn out to watch and to take part.

And, if they see something that needs a community assault to fix, they lead the assault.

Jerry Green led such an assault.

Every year, Ogden held a Christmas parade to lead off the Christmas shopping season. It usually included Santa Claus, bands, the whole bit, but over the years, it had gotten a bit thin.

In 1961, Green took his 6-year-old son, Tom, to see it. They stood on Washington Boulevard and froze, and what they saw was underwhelming, to say the least: Two police cars came by, Santa was on a flatbed truck. He waved, and it was over.

That night, Green had a midnight revelation, with little buildings and lighted Santa castles. He sat up in bed and told his wife to draw sketches of it all.

The next day, he started making phone calls. Every business in town got behind the idea. A warehouse was rented on 29th Street. Hundreds of volunteers built the first buildings, strung the first lights and decked the first halls.

"I will always be grateful for the tremendous effort put forth by Ogden's retail merchants, the Chamber of Commerce, the civic leaders, the churches, the Junior League, and especially the children," Green wrote later. "We had hundreds of volunteers."

Christmas Village opened in 1962, transforming the Municipal Park to a starlit fairyland. It remains, with Pioneer Days, the Weber and Davis county fairs, and dozens of school theatrical productions, a major symbol of what community can achieve.

■ **LEFT:** Ogden Rodeo Band on the steps of the Municipal Building, circa 1955. The band played for the rodeo, parades and concerts in the park during the 1950s. Art Agee, director, is in the front row on the left. Other members: Vern Harrop, trumpet; Michael Pantone, clarinet; Amedio DePierro, clarinet: Hazel DePierro, french horn: A. C. Cook, double euphonium; Stu Eccles, euphonium; Francis Barton, snare drum; Otto Nye, trombone; Paul Wheeler, saxophone; Prentice Agee, trumpet; Ed Holbrook, trumpet; Dick Orrick, drums; George Simpson, trombone; Art Partington, clarinet; and Earl Thompson of the Musicians Union. *Courtesy of Lowell Marriott Harrop*

■ **RIGHT:** Pioneer Days Parade, circa 1942. *Courtesy of Holly Fuller*

LEFT: Union Pacific Railroad Band, 1944. The band played at the Ogden Pioneer Days Rodeo, when dignitaries came to town, at parades and at funerals of fellow employees. The railroad sent the band to Las Vegas to play at the second dedication of Hoover Dam in 1947. *Courtesy of Daneen Swanke*

BELOW: The Cow Jumped Over the Moon float in a parade in 1946. The float was made by students in a commercial art class taught by Farrell Collett. *Courtesy of Leslie Cole*

RIGHT: Cast of an operetta in the 19th Ward, circa 1944. Included are Sandra Call, Maurine Peterson, Dixie Lee Dearden, Dennis Craynor, Beverly Brooks, Marilynn Dearden, Kay Peterson, Sue Evans, Sharon Wheelwright, Charlene Letts, Joyce Fowler, Norma Brooks, Valoy Price, Gordon Kap, Margaret Opeikens, Belle Clark, Elva Craynor, Edith Baker, Sitska Kap, Bessie Cherry, Verla Peterson, Merla Peterson, Nora Duncan, Alta Weaver, Lenora Nelson, June Bond, Verna Call, Jay Cherry, Glada DeFries, Lenore Brown, Karen Green, Carol Call, May Duncan, Emma Jean Stoney, Betty Wilson, Sally Fowler, Wilma Dearden, Alta Craynor, Fae Wilson, Colleen Peterson, Elaine Williamson, Ellen Jacobson, Belle Anderson, Grace Gledhill, Larue Wessler, Idonna Briggs, Ora Forbes, Jenny Cogdell, Evan Green, Shirley Weaver, George DeFries, Verland Carlson, Lynn Gilbert, Malyn Call, LaVar Stanger, Bishop Howard White, Joyce Kilpack and Philo Peterson. *Courtesy of Dixie Holmes*

RIGHT: Parade on Washington Boulevard, circa 1946. *Courtesy of Jason Rusch*

BELOW: Kids getting their torches lit to burn the old Christmas trees, 1947.
Courtesy of Special Collections Department, Stewart Library, Weber State University

ABOVE: Ogden Centennial Parade, 1947. *Courtesy of David Langford*

LEFT: Union Pacific Railroad Marching Band marching in Reno, Nevada, spring 1946. The band was led by Angus "Hank" W. Hansen as drum major and performed in many Western states and at rodeos in Ogden.
Courtesy of Marilyn B. Hansen

121

■ **Above:** Small-scale Pacific Intermountain Express truck at Municipal Park, 1947. David Rusch, age six, is standing on the left. The movie playing at the Orpheum was "Cass Timberlane," starring Spencer Tracy, Lana Turner and Zachary Scott. *Courtesy of David Rusch*

■ **Left:** Weber County's Centennial exhibit in Salt Lake City with two county commissioners and County Agent Christiansen, 1947.
Courtesy of Special Collections Department, Stewart Library, Weber State University

■ **Right:** Ray Minter Drum & Bugle Corp, 1948. Members are on stage at the Pingree School. Marilynn Dearden is in the front on the left; Dennis Craynor is in the front, seventh boy from the right. Dixie Lee Dearden is in the back row, second from the right.

Courtesy of Dixie Holmes

■ **LEFT:** Miss Ogden contest at the Egyptian Theater, Sept. 3, 1948. Contestants included June Bailey, third from the right; Cyrrel Parker, ninth from the right; Wilma Susan Harris, seventh from the the right; Connie Longfellow, fourth from the right; and Shirlee Burnette, fourth from the left. Marilyn Robinson, in the black, won the city and state contests the year prior. She was also a finalist at the Miss America pageant in Atlantic City.

Courtesy of Wilma S. Smith

■ **BELOW:** Playing at the Ogden Golf and Country Club, 1949. Left to right: Bob Stringfellow, sax; Herb Hillier, drums; Ida Marriott, piano; Vern Harrop, trumpet; Maurice Campbell, bass violin; Shorty Ross, vibraharp.

Courtesy of Jerry Harrop and Lowell Marriott Harrop

■ **BELOW:** Float from Washington Terrace in the July 24th Pioneer Days Parade, 1950. Dennis Gladwell is the blond boy in center. *Courtesy of Virginia Gladwell*

■ **ABOVE:** Shorty Ross Orchestra in Berthana Ballroom on 24th Street, 1950. Left to right: Lauro Platon, piano; Valeen Clark Wood, violin; JoAnne Stallings Sontag, violin; Dee Sparrow, bass violin; Roy Critchlow, drums; Betty Ross, vocalist; Shorty Ross, marimba; Vern Harrop, trumpet; and Eva May Chapman, organ. *Courtesy of Jerry Harrop*

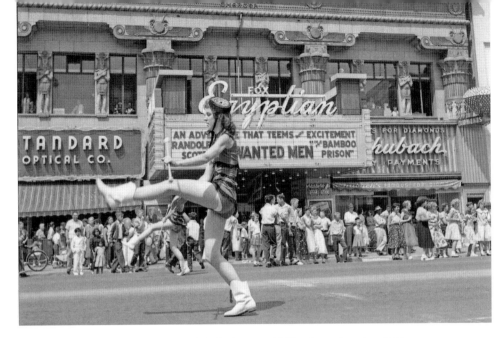

■ **Left:** Parade passing in front of the Egyptian on Washington Boulevard, 1954.
Courtesy of Robert J. Parker

■ **Below:** Huntsville Fourth of July parade float, circa 1958. Left to right: Dan McKay, Sandra McKay, Ben Wilson and LeAnn Wilson. *Courtesy of Doug and Erma Wilson*

GEM OF THE DESERT

■ **Bottom left:** One of Ogden's many drinking fountains, circa 1948. *Courtesy of Jason Rusch*

■ **Bottom middle:** The Cisco Kid in the Pioneer Days Parade on Washington Boulevard, 1958. David, left, and Dean Kap are in front of his horse. *Courtesy of Betty Kap*

■ **Bottom right:** Women at the Ogden Country Club in costume for Red & Blue Day, 1960, left to right: Bonnie Harper, Fern Sliphom, Sadie Pasch, Aliene Pantone and Blanche Bluck.

Courtesy of Sharon Pantone

■ **ABOVE:** Ogden Institute of Religion Men's Chorus at Ogden LDS Tablernacle, 1966. Ladd R. Cropper is the director; May G. Cropper is the accompanist. Members include Jack Arrington, Kent Call, Peter Gallivan, Jerry Harrop, Gerald Hodson, John Marriott and Richard Watkins. *Courtesy of Jerry Harrop*

■ **Right:** Richard Warren and family riding in a stagecoach pulled by palomino horses in the Pioneer Days Parade, July 24, 1966. Richard built the stagecoach himself. *Courtesy of Leslie Liechty*

■ **Below:** People lined up at Santa's Castle in Christmas Village, circa 1965.

Courtesy of Special Collections Department, Stewart Library, Weber State University

■ **Left:** Richard Warren, front, and Noall Hyde driving their chuck wagons with Ponies of America hitch, July 1967. Each night of the rodeo, three chuck wagons would race into Ogden Stadium, build a fire in the painted circle, flip a "wooden" pancake, then race back out of the stadium. *Courtesy of Leslie Liechty*

■ **Below:** Watching the Pioneer Days Parade, 1970.

Courtesy of Bonnie Carrel